British Museum (Natural History)

STARFISHES
and related echinoderms

AILSA M. CLARK
THIRD EDITION

Cover:
Linckia laevigata; photo by Keith Gillett from
Australian Seashores in Colour.

Original figures in the text by Ailsa Clark.

THIRD EDITION

Originally published as *Starfishes and their relations*, first edition 1962.

ISBN 0-87666-466-4

Distributed in the U.S.A. by T.F.H. Publications, Inc., 211 West Sylvania Avenue, P.O. Box 27, Neptune City, N.J. 07753; in England by T.F.H. (Gt. Britain) Ltd., 13 Nutley Lane, Reigate, Surrey; in Canada to the book store and library trade by Clarke, Irwin & Company, Clarwin House, 791 St. Clair Avenue West, Toronto 10, Ontario; in Canada to the pet trade by Rolf C. Hagen Ltd., 3225 Sartelon Street, Montreal 382, Quebec; in Southeast Asia by Y.W. Ong, 9 Lorong 36 Geylang, Singapore 14; in Australia and the south Pacific by Pet Imports Pty. Ltd., P.O. Box 149, Brookvale 2100, N.S.W., Australia. Published by T.F.H. Publications, Inc. Ltd., The British Crown Colony of Hong Kong.

CONTENTS

INTRODUCTION

For a very long time starfishes have been popular symbols of marine life. About 4,000 years ago they featured in the Minoan frescoes of ancient Crete, while today they often appear in newspaper cartoons about the sea-shore. It is true that starfishes belong to one of the few groups of animals that live nowhere else but in the sea. In contrast, the Fishes, Crustacea, Molluscs and other groups of primarily marine forms, have extended their ranges not only into fresh water but also on to the dry land. Even so, within its limits, the sea itself offers a wide variety of different habitats, from intertidal areas with fluctuating conditions to abyssal ones where the enormous pressure and chill temperature are almost constant, from rocky bottoms to others with sand or mud and from cold water to warm, with all sorts of other variables such as salinity and light intensity that combine to produce conditions suitable for one kind of community of plants and animals or another. The starfishes have been quite successful in populating many of the possible niches at the bottom of the sea and well over a thousand species of them exist at the present day. Though some of these are superficially alike, many have obvious differences in shape, size or colour. However, all of them share the outstanding characteristic of the group, namely radial symmetry.

Geometrically this means that they have an imaginary central axis around which the parts of the body radiate in a series of identical sectors, as in a flower like the buttercup. Similarly, the related sea-urchins may be compared with the sphere of the earth with the axis running between the two poles. It is commonly thought that radial symmetry like this is a feature of plants opposed to animals, which are characteristically bilaterally symmetrical, that is with right and left sides forming mirror images of each other. Most animals are of this type, with two sides and at the same time distinct front and rear ends which are specialized in different ways. Starfishes and their relations, on the other hand, have several similar parts radiating from the centre and no special front end. A few other kinds of animals also show this radial symmetry, probably the best-known of these being the Coelenterates, including the jellyfishes and the sea-anemones.

The scientific name for starfishes is Asteroidea, and this is one of the five classes of the group or phylum Echinodermata that have survived to the present day. The four other classes are the Echinoidea (sea-urchins), Ophiuroidea (brittle-stars), Holothurioidea (sea-cucumbers)

Plate I. Representatives of the five classes of Echinoderms: a) the starfish *Asterias*, b) the brittle-star *Ophiothrix*, c) the sea-lily *Endoxocrinus*, d) the sea-urchin *Echinus* and e) the sea-cucumber *Holothuria*. (All but the sea-lily are found in British waters)

6

and Crinoidea (feather-stars and sea-lilies). In former times, as well as representatives of these classes, there also lived species belonging to several others, but these have left no descendants, all of them becoming extinct before the end of the Palaeozoic Era, about 200 million years ago.

The phylum Echinodermata includes exclusively marine invertebrate animals with a skeleton of plates formed mainly of calcium carbonate, a true body cavity or coelom (lacking in the jellyfishes), a free-swimming bilaterally symmetrical larval stage and a radially symmetrical adult form, most commonly with five rays or arms, but still retaining traces of the bilateral origin. A characteristic feature of their structure is the ambulacral system. This involves an internal tube running close to the surface in each radius and giving off side branches in the form of muscular sacs projecting through the body wall. These branches are called the podia or tube feet and form two regular series. Each one has a bulb or ampulla inside the body wall (fig. 2c and f) and this helps to extend or retract the foot by its own contractions or relaxations. The main radial tubes or canals are connected together by a ring canal encircling the central axis of the Echinoderm close behind the mouth. In starfishes, sea-urchins and brittle-stars the ring canal is connected with the external sea-water by a single tube opening through a modified plate in one interradius, though in most holothurians and crinoids the comparable tube or tubes open only internally into the body cavity.

Starfishes and sea-urchins have paired series of ambulacral plates outside the radial canals and these are perforated for the tube feet to pass through. In the starfishes the plates are sunk into the surface to form a groove. The crinoids have an ambulacral groove too, but theirs is more superficial and the plates associated with it are rudimentary.

Originally the function of the ambulacra was to gather food of microscopic size, trap it in mucus and pass it to the mouth by ciliary action. This is still the case in crinoids (and to some extent also in brittle-stars and a few starfishes) but in the other four classes the tube feet have become more or less modified to assist in locomotion and the ambulacra no longer serve primarily for feeding. Their extent varies in the five classes as can be seen from fig. 1.

In the starfishes and most sea-urchins and holothurians, the tube feet operate literally as feet; on a flat surface the individual ones simply step along, their direction being co-ordinated by the nervous system, though there is no regular sequence of movement of the adjacent feet, as there is in segmented animals such as millipedes (fig. 2d and e). Instead the order appears to be quite haphazard. Each tube foot is usually capable of forming a suction cup at its free end, so that if necessary these Echinoderms can cling on to the bottom or climb up a vertical surface.

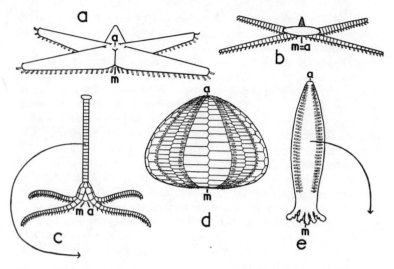

Fig. 1. Diagrammatic figures of representatives of the five classes of Echinoderms in interradial side view [a), b) and c) slightly from above to show the other arms]. a) Starfish, b) brittle-star, c) sea-lily, d) sea-urchin (with spines removed) and e) sea-cucumber; (*m*) mouth and (*a*) anus. The orientation of each is comparable, with the mouth directed downwards. The posture in life is the same as here except for c) and e) where it is indicated by the arrows. (It is possible that the normal alignment of the sea-lily with the mouth upwards is the ancestral one and that it is the other classes which are inverted. However, in our present state of knowledge this is purely conjectural)

On the other hand, some starfishes which live on loose sand or mud have tapering tube feet with no sucking disc at the tip.

However, most brittle-stars and all feather-stars make little or no use of the tube feet in locomotion, so their podia are usually referred to as tentacles. These two kinds of Echinoderms both move either by waving their very flexible arms, or by coiling the tips of these around projections on the sea-bed and pulling themselves along. Only a few brittle-stars use the reduced podia to afford a grip on the substrate or even to assist in climbing.

As for their habits, with few exceptions Echinoderms are adapted for sedentary or even attached life on the sea-bed, some of them burrowing into sand or mud and concealing themselves to some extent, while others live fully exposed.

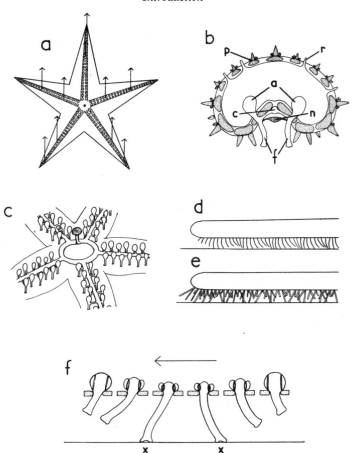

Fig. 2. Diagrammatic figures to show the functioning of the tube feet in starfishes. a) Ventral view of a starfish illustrating the different angles, relative to the long axis of each arm, at which the tube feet must be extended so that the whole body may move in one direction (in this case towards the top of the page), b) transverse section of a starfish arm (the internal organs removed), showing the ambulacral groove and the connections of the feet to the ampullae and the radial canal; (*p*) pedicellaria, (*r*) respiratory tube or papula, (*a*) ampullae, (*c*) radial canal, (*n*) longitudinal nerve and (*f*) tube feet, c) dorso-lateral view of the central part of the canal system showing the tube connecting the ring canal to the dorsal surface in the furthest interradius; in this particular starfish (of the *Asterias* type) the consecutive tube feet are staggered so that there

9

The name Echinodermata, like many other scientific ones, is derived from Greek and signifies 'spiny-skinned'. This refers to the skeleton of calcareous plates formed *under* the skin, in contrast to the skeleton of Crustacea or the shell of most Molluscs, which is secreted on the outside. The sea-urchins are the most obviously spiny-skinned and though their spines may appear to be superficial, they do have a thin covering of skin. The main part of the Echinoderm skeleton consists of plates usually linked together and often bearing spines, knobs, granules or other projections. As a whole, the skeleton shows wide differences in the five classes according to the body form and to the method of locomotion.

Restriction to the sea

The reason why Echinoderms are restricted to life in salt water is probably that there is no impervious barrier between the water circulating through the ambulacral system and the sea-water outside to prevent the inflow of fresh water by osmosis if the external salinity falls below that of the body cells. Echinoderms are consequently very sensitive to 'freshening' of the water and so are kept out of estuaries or seas like the Baltic where the salt content is low. Specimens found on the borderline of such areas are usually stunted in growth and often bloated in appearance owing to excessive water absorption.

---

appear to be four rows when seen from the outside (after Buchsbaum), d) and e) side views of: d) part of a millipede and e) one arm of a starfish, to show the regular sequence of action in the former and the apparently haphazard stepping order of the feet in the latter [only one leg of each pair is shown in d) and the paired arrangement is really far less obvious in e)], f) enlargement of six successive positions of a single tube foot during stepping; the point of contact (x) with the substrate is the same in the two middle figures, the entire body having moved forwards. The stippled part is a section through the ambulacral plate which is perforated for the passage of the tube foot. Within the body the bulb-shaped ampulla is contracted by two pairs of muscles to extend the external tube by pressure of the fluid inside it. Other muscles (not shown here) direct the foot forwards, help in extension and retraction and, if necessary, arch the terminal disc to give adhesion to the substrate.

BODY FORM AND LOCOMOTION

The body of holothurians is unique among Echinoderms both in being cucumber- or even worm-shaped and in being capable of considerable change of shape in most species. The skeleton is reduced to small, usually microscopic, plates or spicules, isolated in the skin and free to slide over one another as the sea-cucumber expands or contracts. In some thick-skinned species these spicules can be very numerous, one estimate[1] from a specimen of *Holothuria impatiens* about eight cm. long, giving a count of over 20 million spicules. Most holothurians have the tube feet concentrated along the five ambulacra running the length of the body and those in the three more ventral ambulacra, which come in contact with the sea bottom, are specialized for locomotion in combination with the powerful longitudinal muscles. There are some holothurians without any tube feet and these propel themselves by muscular contractions, sometimes assisted by gripping the bottom with the tentacles which form a ring around the mouth. This tentacle ring is found in all holothurians but is not otherwise used in locomotion, only for feeding.

The shape of the spicules in the skin is remarkably constant in each species of holothurian and is usually characteristic, though related species may have similar or identical ones. Their forms range from simple or branched rods to perforated plates of many shapes including wheels, baskets, buttons and tables (fig. 3). Each species usually has two distinct types of spicule, flattened ones deep in the body wall and thicker ones nearer the surface with vertical projections giving the skin a rough texture and a grip on the substrate.

In starfishes the ambulacral plates lining the groove along the ventral side of each arm also function as vertebrae, giving support combined with lateral flexibility. Most starfishes also have the body wall reinforced by plates, usually in the form of a semi-rigid network formed by lobed or rectangular plates linked together (figs. 15 and 16). However, there are extreme species either with the skeleton very much reduced and the skin pliable, or, at the other limit, with almost continuous armour-plating. The proportions of the arms are also very variable; some like *Freyella* (Plate VI, fig. j) have long cylindrical arms, while others such as *Tosia* (Plate V, fig. c) have the arms so short that they merge into one another and the body so flat that the form resembles a pentagonal biscuit.

[1]Hampton, *Nature*, vol. 181, pp. 1608–1609, 1958

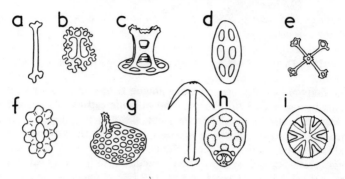

Fig. 3. Spicules of various holothurians. a) Rod, b) rosette, c) table, d) smooth button, e) reduced table, viewed from above, f) knobbed button, g) perforated plate with spire, h) anchor and anchor plate and i) wheel. [Magnification: a), c), d), e), f) and i) approximately × 300, b) × 700, g) × 50 and h) × 150]

Even with a shape like this, *Tosia* is surprisingly mobile and can climb up vertical objects such as pier piles.

The rate of walking has been studied in several species of starfish. It varies considerably and probably averages about fifteen cm. a minute (or ten meters an hour, if the starfish kept going for this length of time).

Brittle-stars differ from starfishes in having the arms sharply marked off from the body or disc, which is soft with only a thin covering of scales or even bare skin over the top. The arms, in contrast, are almost solid, slender and cylindrical, with an internal series of vertebra-like plates and an external sheathing of four longitudinal series of flattened plates. Being so narrow, the arms are much more flexible than those of starfishes, particularly in the horizontal plane. They are firmly joined together at the base by a strong framework around the mouth. The ambulacra run along the ventral side of each arm as in the starfishes, but there is no external groove, the midline being covered by the ventral arm plates, while the tentacles emerge through pores at the sides. Each pair of tentacles corresponds to one ventral and one dorsal plate with a laterial plate on each side carrying a vertical series of usually projecting spines. Brittle-stars move by waving the arms in a rowing action, either two or four of them working in pairs, with the odd arm projecting in front or trailing behind and sometimes helping the movement by a waving motion of its own or by grasping and pulling (fig. 4a). The arm spines, sometimes also the tentacles, may assist by getting a grip on the bottom.

Quite fast speeds (for an Echinoderm) can be reached by this means, up to about two meters in a minute (equivalent to 120 meters in an hour).

The sea-urchins have no projecting arms, the skeleton being modified into a rounded test or shell of flattened plates, joined together at the edges and enclosing a more or less spacious body cavity. The shape of the test is roughly spherical with some degree of flattening in most regular sea-urchins. In the irregular cake-urchins the flattening is much greater and the form almost discoidal, while the heart-urchins are elongated horizontally and more or less egg-shaped.

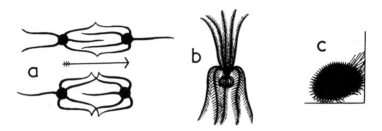

Fig. 4. a) Two brittle-stars moving to the right, the upper with one pair of arms 'rowing', the lower with two pairs, b) feather-star swimming, with one arm of each pair on the downward stroke and the other on the upward, c) sea-urchin starting to climb a vertical surface, the tube feet stretching out to gain a hold

The numerous spines fit on to the outside of the test by ball and socket joints, the 'balls' being knobs on the test, often arranged in regular vertical and horizontal series, while the sockets are at the bases of the spines. The size of the spines ranges from the large 'slate-pencils' of the tropical *Heterocentrotus* (Plate VIII, fig. g) and the very long slender ones of *Diadema* (Plate XV) to the tiny, hair-like spinelets of the cake-urchins.

Apart from having a protective function, the spines usually play a large part in locomotion. Those of regular sea-urchins can be moved like multiple stilts by the muscles at their bases. In the irregular species the much smaller and more closely-placed spines are rhythmically co-ordinated for shovelling through loose sand or mud.

Most regular sea-urchins also use the tube feet to some extent. Since only the lowest ones are normally close to the substrate, most of them are enormously extensible, much more so than in starfishes. They can stretch out, attach their terminal sucking discs and by a combined

13

effort, often helped by the levering action of the spines, pull the body along. The power developed in this way is demonstrated by the fact that quite a bulky urchin, such as *Echinus esculentus*, can climb up the smooth, vertical wall of an aquarium by means of its feet alone. Others, like the tropical *Colobocentrotus* (Plate VIII, fig. e) can cling like limpets on surf-pounded rocks by means of the numerous tube feet concentrated on their lower sides.

In a few sea-urchins even the teeth may be used to pull the body along, particularly when they are stranded in the open air.

The speeds reached vary according to the method of locomotion. The highest estimate for tube feet alone is about 15 cm. a minute or ten meters an hour, whereas stilt-walking on the spines may give a rate of about three cm. a second or a hundred meters an hour, supposing it was kept up.

Finally the crinoids, like the brittle-stars, have well-defined cylindrical arms, but these usually number ten or more, in extreme cases over a hundred, although a very few species have only five. The crinoids differ too in having the arms jointed in such a way as to allow vertical rather than horizontal bending. Most of the free-living feather-stars are quiescent for much of the time, but *Antedon* and its relatives can swim in short bursts by flapping the arms with the alternate ones beating in unison. Probably a distance of little more than a meter is covered in any one spell of action. Some of the large tropical species, particularly those with many arms, move only very slowly by crawling. As for the deep-water sea-lilies, their behaviour in life is unknown. Some are certainly attached permanently to the bottom but others with cirri or grasping organs on the stalk (Plate I, fig. c) may be able to move about to some extent. Unfortunately when dredged up from the depths, their stalks are nearly always broken.

The mass of the crinoid skeleton relative to the soft parts is greater than in any other surviving group of Echinoderms. Superficially crinoids resemble brittle-stars in having the digestive organs restricted to a central disc, supported on a framework linking the bases of the arms. But in the crinoids the centre of the framework is solid and the mouth opens on the upper side of the disc. The cup-like framework is mounted either on the top of a long stalk (in the sea-lilies) or on a single plate equivalent to the topmost stalk segment and called the centrodorsal (in the feather-stars). The centrodorsal usually bears a number of cirri for attachment similar to those along the stalks of some sea-lilies. The greatest difference from the other living Echinoderms is that the crinoids are inverted in their orientation so that the mouth and ambulacral grooves along the arms are on the upper and not the lower surface, as shown in fig. 1.

SYMMETRY AND ORIENTATION

The radial symmetry found in adult Echinoderms differs from that of sea-anemones and jellyfishes in being pentamerous, that is commonly based on five rays (or arms) rather than on four or a multiple of four. Except for rare abnormalities, there are five radii in sea-urchins and holothurians. As for brittle-stars, the great majority normally have five arms, though a few have six and rare exceptions up to nine. Among the crinoids too, most species have five radial plates, each of which gives rise to a series of jointed segments, sometimes forming a single arm but more often branching near the base into two or more. (The very few exceptions to this have ten radials and either ten or twenty arms.) Among the starfishes, however, there are a number of divergences from the rule of five. Even in some species which normally have five arms, individuals may be found with four or six, sometimes even more. For instance, the large West Indian *Oreaster reticulatus* (Plate II), has from four to seven arms. This variability spoiled the early attempt by Johann Linck in 1733 to classify starfishes according to the number of their arms, since he was forced to include species like *reticulatus* in several distinct 'genera'. Even so, Linck's arrangement was better than that of Linnaeus (the founder of our modern binomial nomenclature) who, in 1758, included all the starfishes then known, as well as some brittle-stars and even feather-stars, in the single genus *Asterias*.

Many starfishes, however, are normally multi-rayed and rarely, if ever, have as few as five arms. The best known of these is probably the European sun-star, *Solaster papposus*, which usually has about twelve arms, although they vary in number from eight to fifteen. The sun-star of the west coast of South America, *Heliaster*, may have over forty arms while *Labidiaster* from the Southern Ocean has up to fifty.

In most of the genera with very large numbers of arms like the last two, the number actually increases with size, additional young arms growing between the older ones at intervals around the edge of the disc-like body. Young specimens of *Labidiaster* with a diameter of about 30 mm. (about $1\frac{1}{4}$ inches) have about 15 arms, but by the time that they reach their full size of about 70 cm., the number may be trebled.

Some other multi-rayed starfishes habitually reproduce themselves asexually by spontaneously dividing into two, each half then regenerating the missing part of the disc and the lost arms. A shallow-water Mediterranean species, *Coscinasterias tenuispina*, divides like this; it usually has seven or eight arms, but specimens with all the arms identical in size are rarely found owing to the repeated divisions they undergo. A few

Plate II. The number of arms in starfishes: a) to d) four specimens of the West Indian starfish *Oreaster reticulatus*, each with a different number of arms, though five is the most common; e) the European sun-star *Solaster papposus*, f) the antarctic multi-rayed *Labidiaster annulatus*, with additional young arms being formed between the older ones

brittle-stars, like the commonly six-armed tropical *Ophiactis savignyi*, also reproduce in this way, most individuals having three arms larger than the other three.

As already mentioned, the larval forms of Echinoderms are bilaterally symmetrical. The change to a radial shape takes place during a drastic metamorphosis. However, in none of the adult forms is the external radial symmetry quite perfect, although it may appear superficially so in starfishes, brittle-stars and regular sea-urchins. Even in these it is marred by the single eccentric opening of the water circulatory system which is called the sieve plate or madreporite. In the sea-urchins this is a modification of one of the group of five interradial genital plates in the middle of the upper surface, while in brittle-stars it is one of the five oral shields on the lower surface. In the starfishes it is also placed interradially, but here it is a special plate situated on the dorsal surface with nothing corresponding to it in any of the other interradii (except in a few multi-rayed starfishes which may have one or more supernumerary madreporites, though even then some of the interradii are without). The crinoids have no madreporite but their radial symmetry is modified by the fact that, unlike other Echinoderms, the mouth as well as the anus is situated on the upper surface, so that one of these two openings, usually the anus, must be off-centre. In all the Echinoderms it is possible to imagine a plane bisecting the body and passing through the madreporite (or anus), the two halves so divided being mirror images of one another and the whole animal bilaterally symmetrical. Also any specimen can be orientated to match another by aligning both of them with the madreporite (or anus) in the same relative position. For the sake of comparison, the different rays or arms can then be allotted letters or numbers with respect to one or other of these apertures. The simplest system gives the letters A to E to the five radii, while the interradii become AB, BC, CD, DE and EA. By this method, radius A is the one opposite the interradius which contains the madreporite (in starfishes, brittle-stars, sea-urchins and those holothurians that have an external water pore) or opposite the anal interradius in crinoids. The subsequent letters are allotted to the other radii, working clockwise from A while viewing the Echinoderm from the oral (mouth) side. From the opposite side the sequence is anticlockwise.[1]

[1]Another system commonly used by sea-urchin specialists, is based on the antero-posterior plane of the irregular echinoids. It involves the roman numerals I to V for the radii and arabic ones 1 to 5 for the corresponding interradii to the right of or clockwise from each radius, again in oral view (figs. 5b and 7). Radius B is number I by this system and A is V. In regular urchins interradius CD with the madreporite becomes 2, but in the irregular species the madreporite shifts during early development into the posterior interradius 5.

17

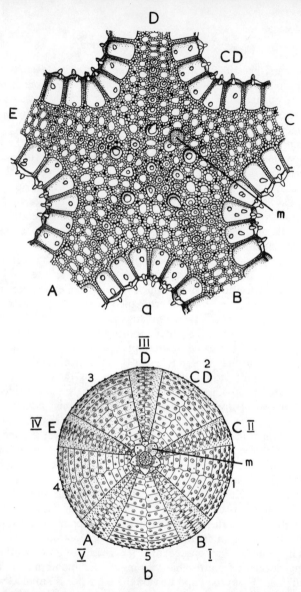

Fig. 5. a) Disc and arm bases of starfish *Calliaster childreni* in dorsal view,
b) sea-urchin *Echinus esculentus* in dorsal view (the divisions between the
apical plates and between the ambulacral and interambulacral series of
plates over-emphasized for the sake of clarity), c) disc and arm bases of
brittle-star *Amphiura chiajei* in ventral view and d) disc and arm bases of
feather-star *Antedon bifida* in ventral view (i.e. from the upper or oral
side), from a preserved specimen, the pinnules being mostly contracted
over the arms rather than extended as in life. In each case, the orientation

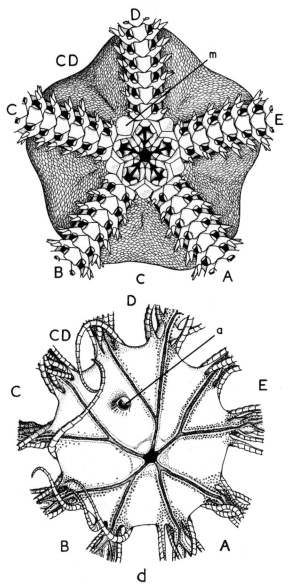

with respect to the madreporite (*m*), or in d) the anus (*a*), is shown by the letters A to E (in the sea-urchin also by numerals), this plate or opening being situated in interradius CD in each case. The anticlockwise sequence in a) and b) is due to the inverted view, from the side opposite to that including the mouth (the aboral side), in comparison with c) and d). In this figure and the two following, each drawing is arranged so that radius D is uppermost, for the sake of the irregular echinoids in figure 7, which thus have the anterior end uppermost

19

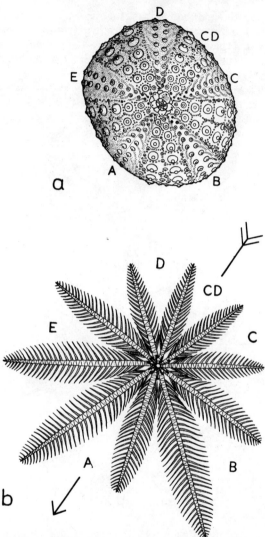

Fig. 6. a) Test of sea-urchin *Echinometra* in dorsal view, without spines, to show the elongation through radius B and interradius ED (or radius 1 and interradius 3 by the numerical notation) and b) diagrammatic representation of dorsal view of feather-star *Comatula pectinata* showing the relative elongation of most of the ' anterior ' arms (i.e. those corresponding to the side of the disc opposite the anus), [after A. H. Clark]

By orientating different individuals in this way it is possible to investigate whether a species has any other structural modifications or even a bias in its behaviour that is constantly aligned with respect to any one radius or arm. For instance, some tropical sea-urchins such as *Echinometra* have the test distinctly oval in dorsal (or ventral) view and this elongation is always in the same plane with respect to the position of the madreporite (fig. 6a). Also a few feather-stars, notably of the genus *Comatula*, have some of the arms on one side of the disc longer

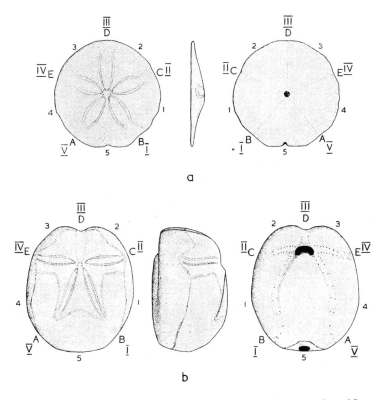

Fig. 7. Denuded tests of: a) Cake-urchin *Echinarachnius parma* from Nova Scotia and b) heart-urchin *Protenaster australis* from Tasmania in (left to right) dorsal, side and ventral views, showing the petaloid arrangement of the dorsal ambulacral pores, the genital pores in the centre (reduced to four in both these species), the anus at the posterior end (i.e. lowermost) and, in b), the mouth towards the anterior end. The narrow dark bands in b) are the fascioles.

than those opposite them, those between being intermediate in size. *Comatula* does have a corresponding orientation in its behaviour since it tends to move with the longer arms in front and the shorter behind. If its progress is blocked then it rotates itself before moving off again, still with the longer arms leading. A few starfishes, such as the multi-rayed Pacific *Pycnopodia*, also show a definite orientation, the arms of one side, though not distinct physically, habitually going first. However, such dominance of one side is rare among those Echinoderms that have the radial symmetry more nearly perfect.

These tendencies to adopt a bilateral form are very slight compared with what is found in the irregular echinoids and the sea-cucumbers, both of which have an instantly recognizable antero-posterior axis and a definite orientation, the mouth usually towards the front and the anus always posterior. The more or less flattened cake-urchins or sand dollars still have the mouth in the centre of the lower surface but in the heart-urchins it has shifted well towards the front. In the development of heart-urchins, at the moment when metamorphosis is completed and before the plates have become firmly sutured together, the shape is already distinctly bilateral. However, this is much less marked than in the adult, indicating their origin from ancestors of regular form. The outline of the test is nearly round and the mouth and anus are both almost centrally placed on the lower and upper surfaces respectively, but in a short time the two openings change their relative positions, the mouth shifting forwards and the anus to the rear.

In the holothurians these two main apertures are usually still in their original positions opposite each other although the body is greatly elongated in between. Holothurians have accordingly adopted the habit of lying with the main axis horizontal instead of vertical and of moving with the mouth end in front. This change in orientation might be compared with a sea-urchin which has become enormously tall and narrow and has toppled over sideways. In most holothurians the lower surface, consisting of three radii or ambulacra, is specialized for creeping by great development of the tube feet, usually accompanied by flattening of the body, even to the extent of forming a snail-like foot or sole in some species.

When orientating holothurians for comparison with the other Echinoderm classes, the mid-ventral radius is termed A and the others similarly lettered clockwise in oral (or in this case front) view. This is in accordance with the location in the mid-dorsal interradius CD of the water pore or equivalent of a madreporite, although such a pore is only found in a few holothurians. Otherwise the CD interradius is distinguished by the position in it of the single genital opening, this class

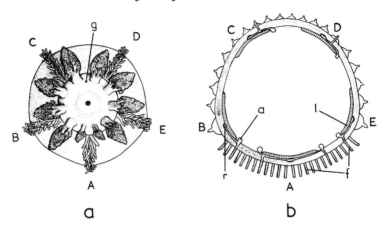

Fig. 8. a) Front, or head-on, view of a sea-cucumber, *Cucumaria planci*, greatly foreshortened, in which the dorso-ventral specialization is limited to the reduction of the two ventral-most of the ten tentacles; the five double rows of tube feet are seen receding along the sides of the body; (*g*) genital opening, and b) diagrammatic transverse section of a species of *Holothuria* with the ventral tube feet developed interradially and the dorsal ones reduced to papillae, and mounted, in this species, on wart-like swellings; the five internal longitudinal muscles are also seen in cross section; (*a*) ampulla, (*l*) longitudinal muscle, (*r*) radial canal and (*f*) tube feet.

of Echinoderms being unique in having the genital organs suppressed in all but the dorsal interradius.

With the development of a ring of tentacles around the mouth, specialized for food gathering and with some sensory function, the holothurians have a nearer approach to a head than any other Echinoderm.

The modification of the irregular echinoids and sea-cucumbers to a bilateral form is a reversion, since Echinoderms are believed to have originated from bilaterally symmetrical animals; the radial symmetry is therefore secondary and the bilateral form of these two groups is tertiary. This theory of their ancestry is supported by the fact that Echinoderm eggs develop into bilateral larvae utterly unlike the radial adult (compare the starfish shown in the frontispiece with fig. 10a), into which they change by a metamorphosis much more complex than that of the amphibian tadpole. So radical is the change that the upper and lower sides of the adult do not correspond to the dorsal and ventral sides of the larva but to its right and left sides.

23

Starfishes and related echinoderms

This different orientation of larva and adult has led some zoologists to reject the terms 'dorsal' and 'ventral' when describing adult Echinoderms and to substitute such words as 'aboral' and 'oral'. The matter is further complicated by the inverted orientation of the crinoids and the sideways one of the holothurians in comparison with the other three classes. It is difficult to be consistent about the terms to be used. In many ways 'oral' and 'aboral' seem to be most favoured but they may be confusing in some cases; for one thing 'aboral' and 'adoral' have been used sometimes in place of 'proximal' and 'distal', in which cases they could both be referring to two sides of a structure situated entirely on the 'aboral' side; also in starfishes and brittle-stars the jaw plates are called oral plates and are therefore difficult to distinguish from the other plates of the 'oral' or ventral side. In any case when dealing with holothurians the term 'anterior' and 'posterior' are much clearer in meaning than 'oral' and 'aboral' and it is still necessary to find words descriptive of the upper and lower sides. In the present work therefore, the familiar terms 'dorsal' and 'ventral' are used for starfishes, sea-urchins,[1] brittle-stars and holothurians, in each case signifying the sides which are respectively uppermost and lowermost in life. Only in the completely inverted crinoids are these untenable and here 'upper-' or 'lower-most in life' are specified.

Radial symmetry is a form particularly suited to the sessile way of life and was almost certainly evolved together with the adoption of an attached habit. It is also found in many of the Coelenterata, including the sea-anemones, corals and hydroids. Although the few surviving species of sea-lilies are the only present-day Echinoderms which are attached, most of the extinct classes included mainly stalked forms, though a few were free-living (probably secondarily). The radial shape is also suited to the sedentary life led by most Echinoderms, but at the same time it imposes a limitation on their potentialities, particularly with regard to the development of elaborate sense organs controlled by concentrations of nervous tissue. The same is true of other sedentary animals such as the bivalved Molluscs, which have little centralization of the nervous system unlike the active, prey-seeking Cephalopod Molluscs such as the Octopus and Squid, which have a very specialized head with highly developed sense organs and a complex mass of nervous tissue amounting to a brain.

The burrowing habit coupled with the absence of necessity to chase their food, has limited the nervous development of the irregular echinoids. However, in some holothurians the same reversion to a bilateral form could mean that the way is opened for an advance in this

[1]Whatever the terminology, the upper and lower 'sides' of the regular sea-urchins are not clearly defined since they merge into each other, usually with a continuous curve, neither being wholly horizontal.

field. A number of holothurians are probably capable of short-term swimming, calling for some degree of sensitivity and quick response to changes in their surroundings, though others have adopted the mentally less exacting burrowing habit.

In general, the Echinoderm nervous system consists of a ring around the mouth from which nerves pass along the radii, together with a plexus or nerve net of cells and processes in the skin, tube feet and other superficial organs; in addition there is a second plexus motivating the muscles of the body wall in starfishes, besides nerves to the digestive system and other structures. The four other groups of Echinoderms show variations in the relative development of the different parts of this loosely integrated system. Since it is so decentralized, the severed arms of starfishes or pieces of holothurians for instance, can survive, at least for a short time, moving about and responding to stimuli. The central nerve ring functions mainly to co-ordinate the actions of the separate arms or radii.

DEVELOPMENT

Animals of sessile or sedentary habits tend to suffer from overcrowding and competition for food unless their life histories include a stage especially adapted for dispersal of the offspring. Many such bottom living (benthic) animals, including the majority of Echinoderms, have a pelagic larva, that is one which lives free of the bottom, swimming in the open sea. Since the size is very small at this stage, the length usually little more than a millimetre, the larvae cannot make any significant headway against ocean currents, unlike fishes or squids, so they form part of the plankton.[1] Although having the advantage of extending the range of the species, this planktonic phase also has two great disadvantages. For one thing, the larvae are liable to be carried out of reach of places where the sea-bed is suitable for them to settle down and develop into the adult form and, for another thing, although the microscopic plant life of the plankton offers them a usually abundant food supply, they are themselves sought as food by larger planktonic animals. To counteract such losses during this random distribution period, vast numbers of eggs may be produced; for instance, it has been estimated that about two and a half *million* eggs are shed during a period of two hours by a female *Asterias* when it is spawning.

The presence of eggs in the water stimulates males of the same species (most Echinoderms, having separate sexes) to eject spermatozoa and bring about fertilization. When this has been successfully achieved, each egg divides repeatedly into segments to form an ovoid larva. Escaping from the egg membrane, the larva swims about by means of countless minute cilia arranged mostly in one or more encircling bands. The length of larval life varies not only with the species but also with the prevailing environmental conditions. In summer the *Asterias* larvae, for instance, spend only about three weeks in the plankton before settling down on the bottom, but in winter this stage is prolonged to at least a month and sometimes two or three, though spawning is more or less suppressed in the less favourable season.

Even at the time of hatching, the larvae of the different classes of Echinoderms are already distinct and they soon become specialized in various ways and take on characteristic forms.

[1]This is a collective name for the small or even microscopic plants and animals that drift with the currents and live mainly in the surface waters of sea or lakes where light can penetrate to allow the plant life to carry on photosynthesis.

Larval forms

The crinoid larva is simply ovoid with several encircling belts of cilia. This form has suggested the name doliolaria from its resemblance to the planktonic salp *Doliolum*, which is similarly transparent with

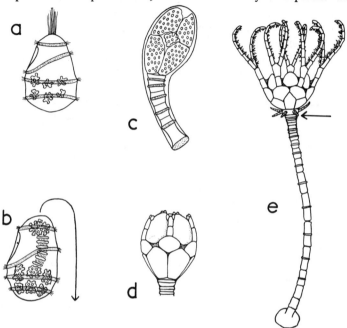

Fig. 9. Development of a crinoid. a) Side view of swimming doliolaria larva with a tuft of long cilia at the anterior end (above) as well as four bands of smaller ones around the body, the second one being distorted by the depression appearing on the left side, called the vestibule; three each of the five basal and five oral plates are shown, b) side view of late doliolaria at the time of attachment, with the stalk plates developing; the arrow indicates the inversion resulting from attachment by the anterior end, c) radial view of young stalked larva, showing two basal and two oral plates of each series, with one of the five radial plates between them, d) radial view of calyx of early pentacrinoid, with the interradial basal plates below and oral plates above (the latter forming a pentagon around the apically placed mouth); each of the radial plates between bears a series of two plates, the outer with the rudiments of a pair of arms, and e) interradial view of later pentacrinoid larva with arms of several joints bearing tentacles, though the pinnules are not yet formed; the cirri are developing around the centrodorsal, above the point where the stalk breaks to free the young feather-star (shown by the arrow)

encircling belts, but these belts are muscles not ciliary bands. The doliolaria has a rather short life compared with other Echinoderm larvae, settling down after only two or three days and attaching itself by the anterior end to the substrate or to weeds or other objects, even to its own parents. The body then elongates considerably with the development of a stalk and at the free end (once posterior) the crown or calyx appears. The mouth forms at the apex and the arms begin to grow out sideways while the stalk elongates further and develops a basal attachment disc which is sometimes lobed. At this stage the larva is called a pentacrinoid (fig. 9e). Most pentacrinoids are less than five mm. long (including the stalk), but a few, notably from cold areas such as the Antarctic, are larger, sometimes about 25 mm. in length. The sea-lilies develop further by enlargement and elaboration of the entire pentacrinoid but the feather-stars break spontaneously at the top-most joint of the stalk and the calyx takes up a free life while the stalk is left to die. Until the life-history of the European feather-star *Antedon bifida* had been followed through, its pentacrinoid was thought to be a dwarfed sea-lily and was given the name *Pentacrinus europeus*.

The larvae of most other Echinoderms have longer free lives and develop complicated forms very different from those they show as adults. Their basic symmetry is bilateral with right and left sides, while they also have the mouth opening towards the front and the anus to the rear. In order to acquire the radial adult form with the mouth in the centre of one side, at one end of the main axis, the larvae have to go through a very complicated and drastic metamorphosis, comparable in magnitude to the change from caterpillar to butterfly but usually accomplished in a much shorter time, in fact within a few hours. So great is the change that it is impossible to recognize from the larva the adult form into which it is destined to develop and this can only be found out by following through the life history. Consequently many larvae have been given provisional names to distinguish them until their true identities could be established.

The main types of larvae correspond to the classes and their 'generic' names are *Bipinnaria* for starfish larvae, *Auricularia* for holothurians, *Echinopluteus* for sea-urchins and *Ophiopluteus* for brittle-stars, the similarity between the last two names being shared by the larvae themselves.

None of the four non-crinoid classes of Echinoderms has such a long-lasting and modified attachment in the larval stage as the pentacrinoid, though some starfishes are temporarily attached by a sucker during metamorphosis. While in the plankton these larvae feed and grow. In order to support the increasing size, the ciliary bands become

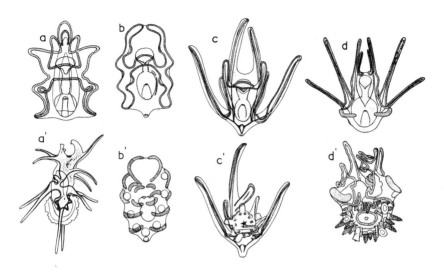

Fig. 10. Development of other Echinoderms, showing a larval stage and the metamorphosis of examples of each class. a) Ventral view of bipinnaria of starfish with two separate bands of cilia looping around the paired lobes, the mouth towards the anterior end (above) leading to the rounded stomach and the anus opening more posteriorly (the cavity like an inverted V is the main coelom) and a′) side view of bipinnaria in the brachiolaria stage, showing the brachiolar arms and sucker for attachment at the anterior end; the adult starfish body is developing posteriorly, b) ventral view of auricularia of holothurian with one continuous band of cilia and b′) ventral view of doliolaria stage of another species of holothurian having a differently shaped spicule at the posterior end; the ciliary band is broken up into short lengths which will rejoin into a series of belts around the body; the spherical objects are transitory elastic balls; in the centre the rudiments of five tentacles have appeared, c) ventral view of ophiopluteus larva of brittle-star with skeletal rods (shown dark but really transparent) supporting the long, paired larval 'arms', c′) ventral view of metamorphosing ophiopluteus, the young brittle-star lying obliquely; the larval arms are being resorbed, d) ventral view of echinopluteus of a regular sea-urchin, differing from the ophiopluteus mainly in the arrangement of the skeletal rods and in the presence of thick ciliary 'epaulettes' around the body towards the posterior end and d′) side view of metamorphosing echinopluteus with the five primary tube feet prominent and the first ten paired feet also developed; the larval 'arms' are being resorbed. [a) After Chadwick, a′) after Mead, b), b′), c) and c′) after Mortensen, d) and d′) after MacBride]

elongated and convoluted or extended out on to lobes or 'arms' of the body. Since the plants and animals of the plankton rise and fall in the upper layers of the water with the daily waning and waxing of the light, the larvae have to be able to swim well enough to keep level with their food and to save themselves from sinking prematurely to the bottom.

The bipinnaria larva of starfishes (fig. 10a) has two separate bands of cilia, a short pre-oral band as well as a main post-oral one supported on several pairs of larval 'arms'. These 'arms' may be very long by the time of metamorphosis when, in some species, a special modification of additional 'brachiolar arms' and a sucker are developed at the anterior end to attach the larva after it has sunk to the bottom. The rudiments of the five (or more) true arms of the adult develop from the coelom towards the posterior part of the larval body particularly on the right side, in such a way that this side becomes the dorsal (or aboral) side of the adult while the larval left side becomes the ventral. The larval 'arms' are resorbed (or rarely, shed) and the original bilateral symmetry is almost completely lost.

The auricularia larva of holothurians is superficially not unlike a bipinnaria, having similar larval 'arms' or lobes unsupported by skeleton, though it differs in having only a single, continuous, ciliary band. But as development proceeds, instead of elongating, the 'arms' are reduced and the convoluted ciliary band divides into several separate encircling bands, so that it too resembles *Doliolum* and has been called a doliolaria (though this does not imply a close affinity with the early crinoid larva). As well as changing its form, the holothurian larva also modifies its behaviour—at least one species has been observed to give up the straightforward swimming of an auricularia and start spinning

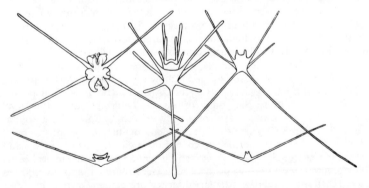

Fig. 11. Some bizarre forms of plutei, all of echinoids, except for the one at lower left which is an ophiopluteus

like a top after turning into a doliolaria. The first sign of the adult form
within the larva is the formation of five lobes from the coelom which
give rise to the primary tentacles.

Finally, the pluteus of sea-urchins and brittle-stars differs in having
skeletal rods supporting the larval 'arms' (fig. 10c and d) and these
'arms' may be enormously long in some species (fig. 11). The adult
body again develops sideways relative to the orientation of the larva and
the larval arms are resorbed and their skeletal rods modified, or sometimes shed, at metamorphosis.

It must be emphasized that these brief notes cover only the most
common types of larvae and the usual course of development in each
of the classes. The larvae themselves vary from one family, even from
one species, to another and some phases of the development may be
extended, curtailed or even totally suppressed. Among the starfishes,
the bipinnaria of *Astropecten* resembles that of *Marthasterias* shown
in fig. 10a but it metamorphoses directly without a brachiolaria stage
such as that of the *Asterias* larva in fig. 10a'. Another starfish, *Luidia*,
has a very peculiar bipinnaria with two huge anterior lobes. One of
these *Luidia* larvae has established a record length for a bipinnaria
of about twelve mm. A few auricularias also attain a similar large size,
in which case the edge of the body with its single ciliary band becomes
elaborated into a complicated frill to support the greater weight. Other
holothurians develop directly into a doliolaria, omitting the auricularia
stage altogether. As for the pluteus, some of the more extraordinary
forms are shown in fig. 11. The central one with the long posterior
'tail' is of a heart-urchin, while the one (lower right) with all the 'arms'
except a single enormous pair suppressed, is of a species of *Diadema*.
The ophiopluteus (lower left) similarly modified is an extreme form of
Ophiothrix larva, though other species of the same genus are much less
divergent. The two plutei shown in fig. 10c and 10d have some resemblance but the larvae of the irregular cake-urchins such as *Echinocyamus*
are very much more like the ophiopluteus of *Ophiura* shown here than
is the echinopluteus of the regular *Psammechinus* given as the echinoid
example, having evolved on convergent lines.

Modified development

Although the majority of Echinoderms of all five classes have
planktonic larvae like these, there are many species in which the free-
living stage is abbreviated or even eliminated altogether from the life
cycle. Instead, a smaller number of larger eggs is produced and these
develop directly into the adult form, or, in the case of such feather-stars,
into the pentacrinoid. The eggs of these species contain enough yolk

31

to sustain them through metamorphosis without the necessity of feeding as larvae. Usually they are shed into the water and left to take their chance of survival, but a number of Echinoderms, particularly species living in polar seas, have evolved the habit of brooding their young in different ways, giving a measure of protection, in a few cases even some nourishment, during the most vulnerable period.

The genital organs or gonads of crinoids are situated on certain of the serially arranged pinnules branching off from the arms. In the species which are brood protecting, the females have a marsupium or pouch alongside the ovary in which the large eggs develop into embryos. These escape from the pouch and attach themselves almost immediately, sometimes even to their mother or to another nearby adult; there they develop into pentacrinoids. In the antarctic species *Phrixometra nutrix*, the pentacrinoid even becomes attached inside the brood pouch, the calyx on the free end of the stalk growing out through a slit in the wall.

Some holothurians have the interesting habit of brooding their eggs in individual pockets in the skin of their backs, rather like the toad *Pipa*, while others have larger pouches each containing several embryos. The pouches have no connection through to the body cavity so that the eggs are presumably shed into the water via the oviducts and pushed into the pouches by the tentacles or anterior tube feet of the mother.

A few other holothurians incubate their young in the body cavity itself, but it is not yet known how the eggs are fertilized in such species. The problem of fertilization also raises itself in connection with one species of starfish which broods the eggs in pockets of the stomach, facing us with the additional question of how the eggs manage to avoid being digested.

Nearly all brittle-stars have internal sacs or bursae into which the several gonads shed their products. These usually open ventrally by a slit on each side of each arm and it is an easy step to brood-rearing for the eggs to be retained in the bursae and to undergo development there, though in a few species the embryos are actually retained in the ovaries. The large antarctic brittle-star *Ophionotus hexactis* (Plate IIIa) is often found with the disc distended by several relatively huge young, with disc diameters of up to about ten mm. and coiled arms about 25 mm. long, while the mother's disc is less than five cm. in diameter. There is usually only one young brittle-star in each ovary. Their escape, presumably via the bursae, has not been observed, but must be a feat involving considerable contortion. Afterwards the ovaries of the mother shrink and are replaced by newly developed gonads. These may include testes as well as ovaries, since *Ophionotus* is hermaphrodite, a condition shared by a number of other brood-rearing brittle-stars,

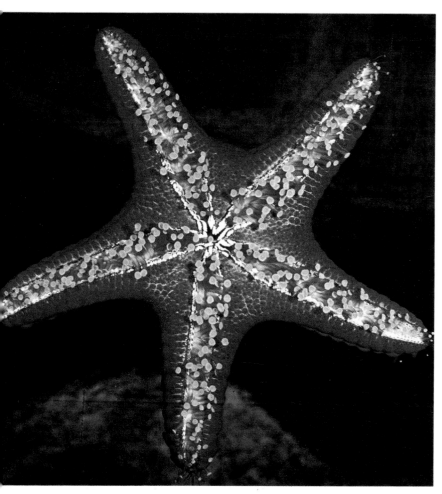

Protoreaster nodosus, viewed from below. This specimen, probably from tropical Australia, shows the tube feet and their conspicuous blue terminal discs. Photo by A. van den Nieuwenhuizen.

in contrast to the majority of Echinoderm species in which the sexes are separate. Self fertilization is probably avoided, as in most hermaphrodite animals, by different timing in the ripening and shedding of the two kinds of genital products. Another hermaphrodite brittle-star, *Ophioceres*, undergoes an interesting alternation of sexes, changing from predominantly male to female, back to male after the young are born and finally ends as a female again. In *Ophionotus*, sperm from another specimen probably reach the eggs in the ovaries through the bursal slits and the bursae. The detailed development of this species is also interesting in that the embryo still forms a larval skeleton although the larval 'arms' which it is designed to support have been suppressed.

Another brittle-star known for a long time to incubate its young is the small cosmopolitan *Amphipholis squamata*. This is particularly interesting because its eggs, which are smaller than is usual in brood-protecting species, develop in the bursae of the parent and seem to obtain some nourishment from the bursal wall. This is then a true case of viviparity, not just of brood protection.

A. squamata shows another feature which is characteristic of species having the brood-rearing habit—namely that the breeding season is extended; in this species it is continuous throughout the year. Most Echinoderms which shed their eggs and give them no further attention, do so only at limited times in the year, when conditions are favourable for the larvae to develop; this is usually the spring in species of temperate seas.

The sea-urchins have no bursae or comparable structures and their rigid tests make it difficult for young with similarly rigid tests and usually erect spines to be brooded internally. However, the habit of protecting the young externally has been developed in a number of species, again mainly polar ones, belonging particularly to the order Cidaroida—regular urchins with massive but spaced primary spines—and to the order Spatangoida or heart-urchins. In these cidarids the young are retained on the surface of the mother, either around the mouth in the centre of the lower side, or around the apical system (where the genital pores open) on the upper side. The corresponding part of the test of the adult may be sunken and usually the primary spines round about are inclined together to form a protective cage for the young. All heart-urchins have their dorsal ambulacral plates modified into five slightly hollowed 'petals' In the genus *Abatus*, which lives in the Southern Ocean, four of the petals are greatly deepened and form brood pouches to shelter the young; viewed from inside the test these appear as very conspicuous bulges (Plate III, figs. c and d).

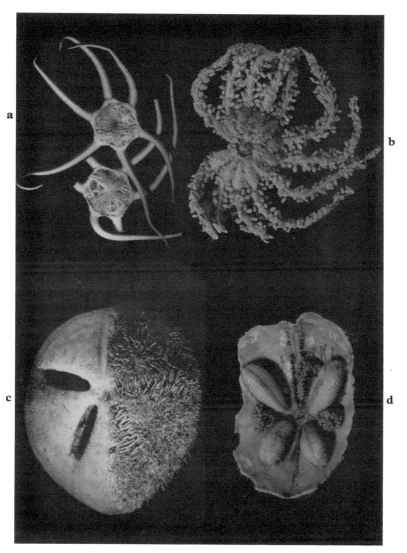

Plate III. Brood-rearing in Echinoderms: a) two specimens of the six-armed brittle-star *Ophionotus* with the disc cut open to show young specimens developing in the very distended ovaries, b) the multi-rayed starfish *Odinella* showing the bulge made at the base of each arm by the formation of a brood cavity (one arm has been removed), c) and d) the upper side of the heart-urchin *Abatus*, showing the brood cavities formed by the bulging inwards of the petaloid areas, c) from the outside and d) from the inside, also showing the ovaries. All these come from the Southern Ocean

Dermasterias imbricata, a smooth North American Pacific starfish, showing the central anus, offset interradial madreporite and groups of respiratory papulae. Photo by Dan Gotschall.

Below:
Fromia sp., a tropical starfish with spaced respiratory pores for the papulae, which show as black spots between the upper plates. Photo by Aaron Norman.

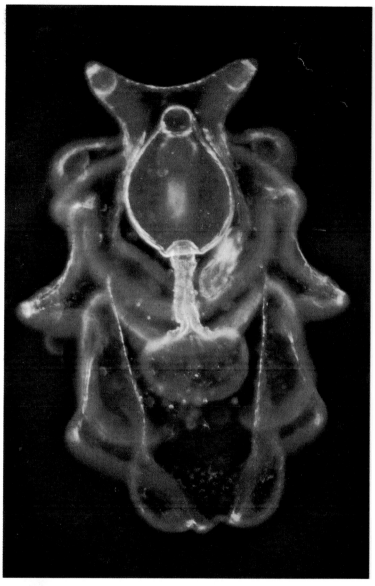

Bipinnaria larva of the starfish *Pisaster ochraceus*. Photo by T.E. Thompson.

Finally, there are many starfishes which also take care of their young to some extent. This may simply amount to their attaching the eggs in sheltered positions on the sea-bed, but often the eggs are protected by the bodies of their parents. Among the long-armed starfishes the usual practise is to hump up the centre of the disc in a straddling position like that adopted when feeding (p. 111). The mass of eggs is housed in the concave space below the mouth formed by the bases of the arms. This position may be kept up for some weeks, during which time the parent is unable to feed. The eggs of such brood-rearing species are usually relatively large and yolky, sometimes more than 2·5 mm. in diameter. Rarely, the individual embryos are attached at the mouth or interradially by a thin cord leading either to a mass of tissue in the middle of the brood, or to a stalk leading from the mouth of the mother. It is not yet known whether this attachment serves to transmit nourishment, or simply to hold the brood together. On the other hand, there are many short-armed starfishes also with the broodrearing habit, and it is more difficult for them to form such a cavity, though the small antarctic species *Kampylaster incurvatus* holds itself with the arm bent downwards and the whole ventral side concave. Most other short-armed forms retain the young instead on the upper surface, since their dorsal plates usually have a central knob or stalk crowned with spinelets, providing shelter for the developing embryos. As the young grow, the plates become displaced to make room for them and the thin skin between is pushed downwards to form a pocket. This habit is carried further in the family Pterasteridae where a supra-dorsal membrane is developed, roofing over the entire surface and supported by the tips of long spinelets mounted on slender stalks, one on each plate. The cavity formed in this way is used by the female to accommodate the young until they have grown to a diameter about a tenth that of the parent, when they escape through a rupture in the membrane. Since several young of different sizes are sheltered at the same time, the dorsal surface of the mother may appear very distorted. In conjunction with this habit, Pterasterids have the genital ducts opening dorsally into the cavity, unlike most other starfishes, particularly those which brood their young ventrally.

Altogether the Echinoderms show an extraordinary range in their development, from those which shed millions of minute, vulnerable eggs at random, to the other extreme where only a few young ones are nurtured to an advanced stage. The only general conclusion is that the number of eggs produced by individuals of each species is inversely proportional to the size and reserves of nutriment of the eggs, or to the extent of parental care that they receive, but is often a combination of both factors.

a

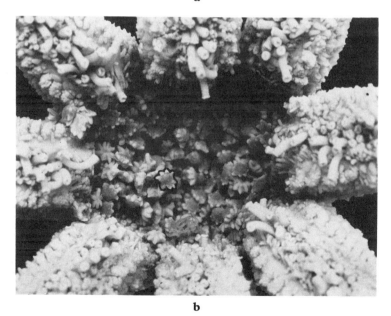

b

Plate IV. Brood-rearing in Echinoderms; temporary brood cavities: a) the sea-urchin *Ctenocidaris nutrix* and b) the starfish *Diplasterias octoradiata*, both with young protected below the mouth either by a lattice of spines or by the humping up of the disc and arm bases. In a) all but the innermost primary spines have been broken off for the sake of clarity; in b) one of the young near the centre has been outlined in black.

Both these species are also from the Southern Ocean

Pteraster tesselatus, a North Pacific starfish; the puffy appearance of the upper side results from the supra-dorsal membrane. Photo by Dan Gotschall.

Patiriella calcar. This asterinid from Australia normally has eight arms, but at least one individual shown here has seven arms. Photo by T.E. Thompson.

Nardoa novaecaledoniae, a long-armed *Nardoa* species from Australia. Photo by Keith Gillett.

INTERRELATIONSHIPS OF ECHINODERMS

This has been the subject of several conflicting theories and is not yet fully resolved. Although one proposal* puts them close to the starfishes and brittle-stars, the 'classical' theory is that the Crinoids are marked off from the rest by the early settlement of the larva and the development of the stalk. This, together with the inverted orientation and many different structural features of the adult, appears to justify their distinction in a separate sub-phylum from the other four classes. The larvae of these four have a number of characters in common, particularly those of the sea-urchins and brittle-stars. However, the direct evidence of the fossil record shows that the brittle-stars arose from a common stock with the starfishes, as the superficial forms of the adults suggest. Unfortunately, the fossil history of Echinoderms is still too incompletely known to be of much help in clearing up the interrelationships of the other classes. The holothurians do not make good fossils and the links between the earliest echinoids and the starfish-brittle-star stock are still missing; possibly such links only existed in the pre-Cambrian Era, more than 520 million years ago, before recognizable fossils were formed. We can only make deductions about their relationships from the comparative anatomy of the available fossil and recent forms and from the physiology and life histories of the survivors.

*Fell and Pawson *in* Boolootian, see 'Suggested further reading'.

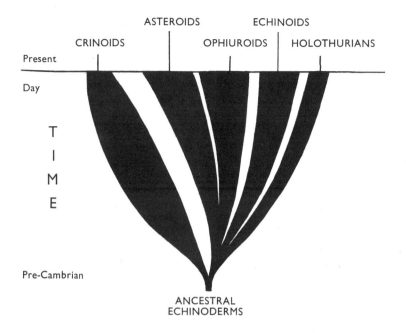

Fig. 12. Family tree showing the classical view of the evolutionary history
of the surviving groups of Echinoderms

A view of the underside of *Marthasterias glacialis*, a carnivorous European asteriid starfish with wreaths of minute pedicellariae around the large spaced spines. Below: a view of the upper surface of the same starfish. Photos by Dr. S. Frank.

Culcita novaeguineae in side view. Some individuals are found even more inflated than this. Photo by Roger Steene.

Plectaster decanus, from southeast Australia, a spinulosan with inconspicuous marginals. Photo by T.E. Thompson.

CLASSIFICATION

Starfishes (Asteroidea)[1]

As with the other Echinoderm class names, the word Asteroid has a Greek origin, being modified from words meaning 'star-form' or 'star-like'. It may be better known in its use for the smaller planetary bodies in the solar system but for about a hundred years has been applied to starfishes. The earlier term 'Stellerides' used particularly by French zoologists such as Lamarck, included some other Echinoderms as well.

At the present time (1977) about 1600[2] distinct species of living (as opposed to fossil) starfishes are recognized. However, only fifteen of these have been found in British waters in depths of less than 100 fathoms (183 metres). This small proportion highlights the narrow geographical ranges of most bottom-living or benthic marine animals such as Echinoderms. Their distribution is limited by the varying composition and topography of the sea-bed, by temperature and pressure differences according to locality and depth, and by other factors such as food supply. In contrast, a pelagic life spent in the open sea free of the bottom, offers more nearly uniform conditions as well as a means of dispersal over a wide range. The only starfish species which are found both in the Indo-Pacific and Atlantic oceans are a few that are limited to great depths where conditions are least variable. Also, their spread from one ocean to the other has been made easier by the wide continuity of the abyssal areas in polar seas.

Specialists on recent starfishes group the known species into about 300 genera and these in turn into thirty families and five orders within the class Asteroidea. Three of the orders, Platyasterida, Paxillosida and Valvatida, include forms with prominent marginal plates reinforcing the sides of the body, in contrast to the Spinulosida and Forcipulatida. The last order is marked off from the rest by the structure of the pedicellariae. These are small, superficial, grasping organs which are

[1]The popular English name ' starfishes ' has been condemned by the late Theodor Mortensen, an eminent Danish authority on Echinoderms, since it wrongly suggests that they are related to the true fishes. He thought that a better name would be ' sea-stars ', in line with the French ' étoiles-de-mer ' and the German ' see-sterne ', as well as with ' brittle-stars ' and ' feather-stars ', the English names for two other Echinoderm groups. However, the term ' starfishes ' is far too well established in the language for there to be any hope of changing it now. At least it is not so misleading as the comprehensive ' shell-fish ' which makes no distinction between groups as different as the Crustacea and the Mollusca.

[2]This estimate was made in 1962 but the number of new species described meantime is probably balanced by a similar number of names rejected as synonyms.

found in one form or another in most species of starfish, as well as in sea-urchins. The function of the pedicellariae has been studied in a few starfishes; they may serve for cleaning as well as defence or offence according to the nature, edible or otherwise, of the objects coming

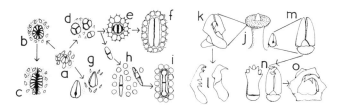

Fig. 13. Enlargements of pedicellariae of various starfishes. a) to d) Paxillosida, e), f), h), i) Valvatida, g) Platyasterida, j) to o) Forcipulatida. a) Simple fasciculate one of an Astropectinid, b) modified fasciculate and c) pectinate of two Benthopectinids, d) granuliform of another Astropectinid, 3) and f) valvate of *Ceramaster* and *Hippasteria*, g) two- and three-valved of *Luidia*, h) and i) 'sugar-tongs' of *Mediaster* and *Ophidiaster*, j) single spine of Asteriid with raised collar of small crossed pedicellariae and a larger straight one near its foot, k) crossed one enlarged, l) single valves of crossed pedicellariae of *Pedicellaster* (left) and *Notasterias* (right), m) straight one enlarged, n) felipedal straight one of *Leptasterias* in two views, o) furcate straight one of *Pisaster*. [Magnifications: a) to e), h) and i) x 12, f) and g) x 5, j) x 10, k), l) and o) x 100, m) and n) x 50]

in contact with them and to the degree of hunger or repletion of the starfish at the time. Sometimes the object is simply seized and held immobile, often by large numbers of pedicellariae, if these are within reach. In addition, the tube feet may help in gripping a large mass like a fish, though it is probably only in the confined quarters of an aquarium that capture of such an active creature is possible. In other instances, the foreign bodies are passed to the tube feet and carried either to the mouth or off to the side where they are rejected. Sometimes contortions of the arms may assist in passing food to the mouth.

The simplest type of pedicellaria is found in some Paxillosidan genera such as *Astropecten*. This consists of several adjacent spinelets, barely differentiated from the rest, but aligned so that their tips can pinch together. The basal muscles are probably modified and co-ordinated to some extent to assist in this grasping action. Such a spine cluster (or fasciculate pedicellaria, figs. 13a and b) may be elaborated by

Culcita sp., a pentagonal oreasterid species of tropical Indo-West Pacific coral reefs, capable of inflating itself to something like a slightly deflated football. Photo by G. Marcuse.

Opposite:
A short-armed oreasterid in side view. Photo by Roger Steene.

having its spinelets or valves tapered to a sharp point and curved inwards, or the spinelets can be arranged in two opposing combs along the edges of adjacent plates (forming a pectinate pedicellaria, fig. 13c).

More often, however, the number of spinelets or valves is reduced to only two or three. This is the case in *Luidia* (fig. 13g), where large and quite specialized elongated pedicellariæ are found. In other genera too the valves may be so modified in shape that their derivation from spinelets is not at all obvious. For instance, they may be short and rounded so that the whole resembles a split granule, or flattened and either long and narrow ('sugar-tongs' style) or short and broad (valvate). In extreme examples of the last type, as in *Hippasteria*, these pedicellariae resemble a pair of closed lips and are often large enough to be easily seen with the naked eye. Valvate ones frequently occur in a parallel series on the first row of ventral plates adjacent to each ambulacral furrow. The sugar-tongs type is usually sunk into a recess in the plate carrying it so that the valves lie flat when opened out (figs. 13h and i).

Some pedicellariae are found in a few members of the Spinulosida, but many have none at all. In the Forcipulatida, believed to be the most advanced order, pedicellariae of a more elaborate type almost invariably occur. These differ in having an additional basal plate integrated with the two valves. The valves themselves may be bent into an L-shape, the two lower halves overlapping and flattened, with the basal piece sandwiched between them, so that they have a scissors action. This is a crossed pedicellaria as opposed to the straight kind, in which the valves do not cross but meet the basal piece at right angles in the same plane. There are further variations on these two kinds, some of them characteristic of single genera or even of species. The valves may have fine or coarse teeth in different positions; sometimes in crossed ones there are a few large fangs near their tips (fig. 13l). The straight ones may have overlapping claws and resemble two cat's paws faced together (hence the name felipedal), or each valve can be forked from near its base (in a furcate pedicellaria). In general, the crossed pedicellariae are small (though there are rare exceptions) and are often mounted in clusters on the skin sheaths around the spines, while the straight pedicellariae are relatively large and are situated between the spines.

Most Spinulosida and all Forcipulatida have a relatively small central disc and almost cylindrical arms with no conspicuous series of marginal plates bordering them. The other orders conversely have the body more or less flattened with usually two rows of marginal plates forming a distinct border around it. The arms may also be very short and merge with the disc, in extreme cases making the outline almost pentagonal, as in *Tosia*. The Spinulosida are intermediate in many ways, including

Plate V. Various starfishes: a) *Lysaster*, in oblique view to show the large marginal plates with cribriform organs between those bordering the body, b) *Ctenodiscus* a mud-feeder, c) *Tosia* with pentagonal body, d) *Luidia* with reduced supero-marginal plates, e) *Benthopecten* with an odd marginal plate and spine in each interradius, f) *Astropecten* seen from below, with tube feet lacking sucking discs, g) *Gomophia* one of the Ophidiasteridae with conical tubercles on the arms and h) *Culcita* with a very inflated body

Iconaster longimanus, a goniasterid from the tropical West Pacific; the large marginal plates alone form the outer skeleton of the arms. Photo by Allan Power from *The Great Barrier Reef.*

Choriaster granulatus, a fleshy smooth Indo-West Pacific oreasterid. Photo by Dr. Herbert R. Axelrod.

Below:
Neoferdina ocellata, a beautifully patterned tropical West Pacific ophidiasterid, the upper marginal plates contrasting in colour. Photo by Allan Power.

starfishes exhibiting both extremes of form, some like *Asterina* being almost pentagonal, while others like *Henricia* have small discs and cylindrical arms.

Some of the exceptions to the usual pentaradiate form have already been mentioned under the heading of symmetry, but there are also wide variations in the shapes of the arms and in the size reached by adults of the different species. While some, such as *Marginaster*, may only grow to a diameter of about ten mm., others like *Marthasterias* (frontispiece) and a few polar species, can reach a span of as much as a meter, though the average is about ten to 12 cm. In scientific work, the size is expressed as the length of the major radius (R) from the centre of the disc to the tip of an arm, since in five-rayed species no two arms are exactly opposite and the diameter can only be an approximation. To obtain an idea of the shape, the ratio of R against r (the minor radius from the centre of the disc to its edge inter-radially) is usually given. In extreme cases the ratio may be as low as 1/1, for instance in the almost bun-shaped genus *Culcita* which is pentagonal but inflated interradially, or as high as 20/1 in some deep-sea forms with enormously long arms and very small central disc. Most often the ratio is about 4 or 5/1.

For sheer bulk, probably the largest starfishes are some of those included in the family Oreasteridae, notably *Culcita* and *Oreaster* itself. The shallow-water West Indian *Oreaster reticulatus* (Plate II) reaches a major radius (R) of nearly thirty cm.; since the disc is both high in the centre and wide across, so that R/r is not much over 2/1, the total volume is considerable. Some other starfishes have longer arms than

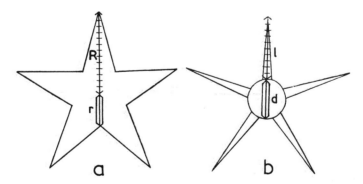

Fig. 14. Diagrams of a starfish a) and brittle-star b) showing the different measurements used in describing them. (R) major and (r) minor radii of starfish, (l) arm length and (d) disc diameter of brittle-star

b

Plate VI. Various starfishes: a) *Peribolaster*, with large paxillae sheathed in thick skin, b) and c) side and dorsal views of *Anseropoda* showing the extreme flattening of the body, d) *Henricia* and e) the related genus *Rhopiella*, f) ventral view of *Porania* showing the channels in the thick skin leading from the margins to the ambulacral furrows, g) the coral reef spiky starfish *Acanthaster* (the size very reduced in comparison with the others), h) *Asterina* the common cushion-star, i) *Pteraster*, the apparent lack of focus due to the soft supra-dorsal membrane roofing over the back, j) the deep-sea Brisingid *Freyella*, showing only the bases of the very long arms and k) the skeleton of *Asterias*

Ophiocoma dentata, an Indo-West Pacific species of the most common coral reef genus. Photo by Allan Power.

this but at the same time the arms are narrow or flattened and the disc is relatively small so that the bulk is not so great.

Another factor contributing to the different appearances of various starfishes is the development of the skeletal plates and their ornamentation or armament. The plates lining the ambulacral furrows on the underside of each arm are always well developed and firmly linked together by joints and muscles. Like the vertebrate backbone they provide support combined with a degree of flexibility. It is the plates of the body wall, particularly the two rows of marginal ones, which are variable. In most of the Paxillosida like *Astropecten* (figs. 15e and f) the marginal plates are massive, while in many Spinulosida, such as *Henricia* (fig. 15l) and in the Forcipulatida the marginals may be only distinguishable by their serial arrangement and instead of defining the lateral limit of the body they are more or less displaced on to the ventral surface. In extreme cases the ventral and dorsal plates merge imperceptibly and the marginals are not apparent at all.

The most common form of the dorsal plates is such that they make an open network, the plates overlapping each other to some extent and leaving space in the meshes between for small, thin-walled sacs or papulae. These serve for respiration and can be withdrawn should conditions become unfavourable. They usually occur all over the dorsal side, and sometimes also around the margins to the ventral side, but in the family Benthopectinidae they are restricted to an area near the base of each arm on the dorsal side.

In some species the network of plates can be seen clearly in the live starfish, but usually it is obscured by a covering of spinelets or other processes, if not by considerable thickening of the skin. In the genus *Porania*, for instance, the skin becomes so thick in larger specimens that the plates can be seen only in X-ray photographs or by dissolving the skin away with chemicals. A few genera related to *Porania* have the plates resorbed and even lost altogether as growth proceeds. Conversely the plates may be so well developed as to form an almost continuous coat of armour, as in some relatives of *Linckia*.

Though the dorsal and ventral plates of *Porania*, deeply embedded in the body wall, may only have a few low tubercles, those of most other starfishes do have granules, spinelets, spines or knobs of some kind. Often, the central part of each plate is raised into a table or a column, which may be tall and narrow in some species. The spinelets or other armament are then limited to the apex of this table or column (fig. 16a) and the basal part of the plate is usually lobed so as to articulate with the neighbouring plates. The columnar type of plate with a crown of spinelets is called a paxilla and is common among genera of the Platyasterida

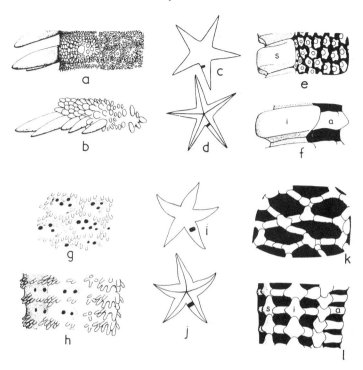

Fig. 15. Structural details of *Astropecten aranciacus* [a) to f)] and *Henricia obesa* [g) to 1)]. a) and e) Enlargements of the black sector in c) showing a supero-marginal (*s*) and the adjacent dorsal plates with spinelets and spines intact and removed, b) and f) enlargements of the sector in d) showing an infero-marginal (*i*) and the adjacent adambulacral plate (*a*), with spines and spinelets intact and removed; g), h), k) and l) similar enlargements of the sectors shown in i) and j). [In b), f), h) and l) the ambulacral furrow is to the right]

and Paxillosida such as *Luidia* and *Astropecten* as well as in some Spinulosida such as *Solaster* and *Pteraster*. The skin sheathing the paxilla is usually thin and inconspicuous, but in the Southern Ocean genus *Perknaster* the whole body wall is thickened and the column and spinelets are buried in it and obscured from sight. A similar development has apparently taken place in *Pteraster* where the upper surface is covered with skin and no spinelets are visible externally. However, in this case the skin has developed as a roof held up by the tips of the very elongated paxillar spinelets forming an extra cavity as described in the preceding section.

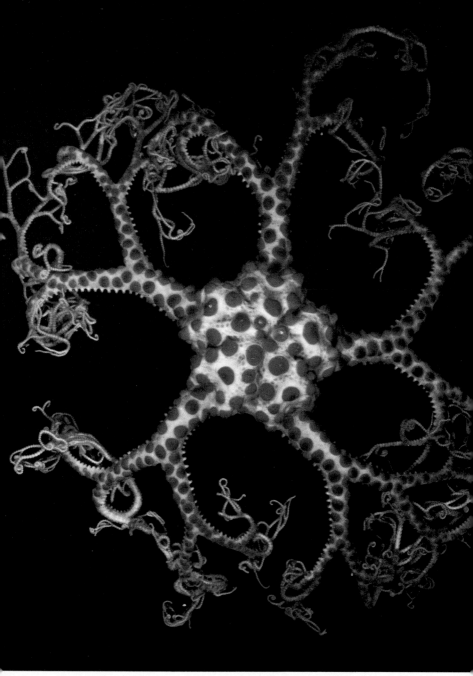

Conocladus amblyconus, an offshore basket-star from southeast Australia having a particularly knobby ornamentation. Photo by Keith Gillett.

Ophiarachna incrassata, from the tropical West Pacific; this is the largest known brittle-star. Photo by Keith Gillett.

Another unusual development of the skin in *Pteraster* is the formation of webs between the spines. There is a web transverse to the ambulacral furrow on each adambulacral plate linking the fan of spines. Also, the outermost adambulacral spine helps to support a longitudinal web along the side of each arm.

The tabular form of plate can be likened to a very squat paxilla. It is particularly common in the Valvatid family Goniasteridae. The raised part is low and wide, usually equal to more than half the total area of the plate and crowned with granules or short spinelets. Often the

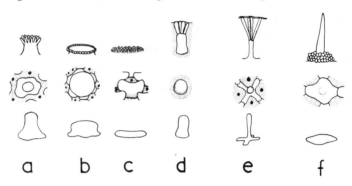

Fig. 16. Details of plates of various starfishes. a) Paxilliform plate of *Astropecten*, b) tabular one of *Tosia*, c) crescentic one of *Asterina*, d) embedded paxilliform one of *Perknaster*, e) elongated paxilliform one of *Pteraster* supporting the roof of skin and f) lobed plate of *Marthasterias*. In each the upper figure shows a lateral view of the plate intact with skin and spinelets, granules or spines, and the middle and lower figures, respectively, dorsal and lateral views of the cleaned plates. [In f) upper, the large spine is surrounded by its sheath of pedicellariae retracted around its base]

granules are crowded, flat-topped and polygonal, forming a continuous pavement with those of the adjacent plates, as in *Ceramaster*. Sometimes, particularly with the marginal plates, the centre of each is naked and the granules are limited to a ring round the edge (fig. 16b). This is the condition of the dorsal plates, and sometimes of the ventral plates as well, in genera such as *Tosia*. The related genus *Goniaster* not only has rings of granules around the plates but also some of the dorsal ones in the radial areas have a large conical knob taking up the whole free surface of the plate.

In both the paxilliform and tabular types of plate the basal part of each one usually extends horizontally in a number of lobes articulating with those of adjacent plates. Alternatively the linkage is made by additional secondary plates.

Many of the Spinulosida and most of the Forcipulatida have simply a network of lobed or bar-like plates without vertical protuberances, although low tubercles, each forming a base for a single spine or spinelet, occur in most of the Forcipulatids (fig. 16f).

A number of different starfishes have some conspicuous spines on certain plates. Among the Paxillosida, this is particularly true of the marginal plates, which are themselves usually outstanding. The deep-sea genus *Styracaster* has a flat, pentagonal body with five narrow arms projecting abruptly, one at each angle. The two series of supero-marginal plates of each arm are in contact dorsally and alternate ones of each side usually bear a large, conical spine. Apart from these, *Styracaster* presents a rather smooth appearance. The related *Lysaster*, shown in Plate V, is similar but has smaller marginal spines. Another deep-sea genus, *Benthopecten*, has a very bristly aspect, all the marginal plates having spaced, spike-liké spines, likewise some dorsal plates also, but these are all dwarfed by five big spines, one in each interradius, arising from unpaired supero-marginal plates.

Of the Forcipulatid families, the Brisingidae is also confined to deep water and most of the genera belonging to it have very long, slender, sometimes needle-like, single marginal spines. In addition the Brisingids are multi-armed and resemble the brittle-stars in having the arms very narrow and the central disc small and round. The superficial skeleton of the arms is usually reduced to a series of transverse ribs in the basal part, and the joints linking the arms to the disc are easily broken. Most Brisingids are very fragile and in some species only the arms are known, no discs having survived the rough treatment of trawling and reached the surface to be preserved for study.

However, deep-sea starfishes are not the only very spiny ones. The shallow-water genus *Acanthaster*, notorious on coral reefs, has a number of very large, spaced, spike-like spines, each up to an inch long and mounted on a tall column; these are scattered over the dorsal surface making a conspicuous defensive armament. *Acanthaster* reaches a diameter of over a foot and has about fifteen arms, so it is quite a formidable-looking starfish. It has another interesting characteristic in that each specimen develops several madreporites. Normally such multiplication is linked in multi-armed starfishes with the habit of spontaneous fission and regeneration, but *Acanthaster* does not reproduce asexually in this way. Some other shallow-water genera which may have enlarged spines include *Luidia, Astropecten* and *Marthasterias*.

Heterocentrotus mammillatus, a tropical Indo-West Pacific species, called the slate pencil urchin because of its massive spines. Photo by Keith Gillett from *The Australian Great Barrier Reef in Colour.*

In contrast to these spinose forms, certain starfishes appear smooth externally, having an almost flush coating either of uniform granules or fine spinelets, as in *Linckia* and *Asterina*, as well as in some species of *Henricia*. Alternatively, there may be a covering of thick skin over the entire surface as already described in *Porania*, though some species of *Porania* may have tubercles projecting on the dorsal side as well as a fringe of marginal spines. In a few of these smoother starfishes the only spines of any size are those bordering the ambulacral furrows on the ventral side.

Between the extremes of spiny and smooth starfishes come a great number of intermediate ones, including the common Forcipulatid *Asterias*, with an irregularly rugose surface owing to the scattering of numerous small spinelets or spines.

The colour range of starfishes is very great; probably various shades of red are the most common since the pigments involved are usually carotenoids, but white, yellow, green, grey and blue are also found. Sometimes there is a pattern of different colours or shades and often the ventral side is paler than the dorsal. A single species may be very variable in this respect, notably *Asterias rubens*, which ranges from yellow to purple.

Brittle-Stars and Basket-Stars (Ophiuroidea)

The name Ophiuroidea is derived from 'Ophis', the Greek for snake and refers to the appearance of the arms in those species of brittle-stars in which the arm spines are small and close-lying. This has also given rise to the alternative popular name of serpent-stars.

The general organization of ophiuroids is similar to that of the asteroids except that the digestive organs are limited to the disc and there is no anus, the excreta being expelled through the mouth. The arms have no large extensions of the body cavity and are narrow from the base.

At the present time (1977) about 2,000 species of living ophiuroids are known, of which sixteen can be found in British waters at depths of less than 100 fathoms (183 metres). One of these, *Amphipholis squamata*, is unique in being almost cosmopolitan in shallow water, ranging from Europe to New Zealand and both sides of the American continent. It is a drab, inconspicuous brittle-star, less than five cm. in total diameter and is often found between tide marks, under stones and among coralline weeds. Though dull in appearance, it has two very interesting habits— it broods its young and also it can make its arms luminous. A more conspicuous species is *Ophiothrix fragilis*, a really brittle brittle-star as its name suggests. It shows a great range of colours as well as a variety of minor structural differences that have puzzled many taxonomists when trying to identify and characterize the species of *Ophiothrix*.

About fifteen families of present-day ophiuroids are recognized and these are arranged in two orders, the Euryalida and the Ophiurida. The Euryalida are distinguished by the articulations of their arm joints, which allow them to coil vertically. Their arms as well as their discs are usually covered with thick skin, but sometimes there are granules or tubercles; in a number of genera the arms actually branch repeatedly. All the Ophiurida have the arms unbranched and nearly always covered with scales or plates; their flexibility is usually limited to the horizontal plane. The two families Ophiomyxidae and Hemieuryalidae overlap to some extent since the Ophiomyxidae have skin-covered arms and the Hemieuryalidae can curl the arms downwards. Nevertheless both are included in the Ophiurida.

Those genera of Euryalida in which the arms branch right from the base, as in *Gorgonocephalus* and *Euryale* itself, are called basket-stars. Preserved specimens often resemble a Gorgon's head when the tendril-like outer branches of the arms form a tangled mass, but when alive and feeding the arms are extended up and outwards and the ramifying branches form an open mesh rather like a basket to catch their small swimming prey. Other Euryalids, like *Trichaster*, have only the outer parts of the arms branching, while in *Asteronyx* they are undivided for their whole length but enormously long and coiling (Plate VII, fig. h).

The order Ophiurida includes the brittle-stars. These number nearly ten times as many species as the Euryalids but superficially they are all rather similar. With few exceptions they have a relatively small, more or less flattened disc, averaging about a fifth of the arm length in diameter while the five arms are almost cylindrical and sharply marked off from the disc.

Among the few species which do have more than five arms, the antarctic *Ophiacantha vivipara* is particularly interesting. Most specimens have six or seven arms, though a few have eight. There is also a very similar but five-armed *Ophiacantha* found with *O. vivipara* in the colder parts of its range, which may prove to be specifically indistinguishable from it. The maximum number of arms for a brittle-star is found in another species of *Ophiacantha*, namely *O. enneactis* from the Bering Sea, though only a single specimen has so far been taken; this had nine arms. Another notable multi-rayed species is *Ophiactis savignyi* from the tropics, normally with six arms. Like several other brittle-stars

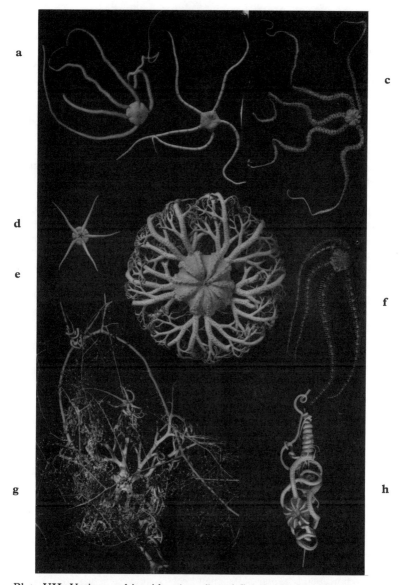

Plate VII. Various ophiuroids: a) to d) and f) brittle-stars, e), g) and h) euryalids. a) Burrowing *Amphiura*, b) *Ophioderma* with close-lying arm spines, c) tropical long-armed *Macrophiothrix*, d) *Ophiura* in ventral view, e) basket-star *Astrocladus*, f) brittle-star *Ophionereis*, g) two euryalids with six unbranched arms and another basket-star seen from below, all clinging to a sea-fan, and h) *Asteronyx* with unbranched but coiling arms

of that genus, as well as a few species in families other than the Ophiactidae, the six-armed condition in *O. savignyi* is correlated with the practice
of asexual reproduction by self division, as described under the heading
of regeneration.

Apart from having more than five radii, few of these species diverge
particularly from the usual brittle-star form. Amongst those that do
depart from it to any great extent are the three species illustrated in
fig. 17. *Ophiopyrgus wyvillethomsoni* has the disc high and conical with
the few large plates firmly joined to one another. *Astrophiura*, on the
contrary, has the whole body extremely flattened and even slightly
concave on the ventral side. Both of these belong to the same family as
the genus *Ophiura*, namely the Ophiuridae (formerly known as the
Ophiolepididae) but *Ophiotholia*, the third aberrant form shown, is
placed in the Ophiacanthidae. In life it may not appear very different
from specimens of *Ophiacantha* itself, but preserved individuals have
the arms aligned vertically upwards and the jaws projecting straight
downwards so that the mouth gapes open and the soft-topped disc is
compressed into a tall cone within the space enclosed by the arms, as
in the figure. To permit this attitude, presumably adopted sometimes
in life as well as in death, the articulation of the skeleton must be modified. The genus occurs in deep water and live specimens have not yet

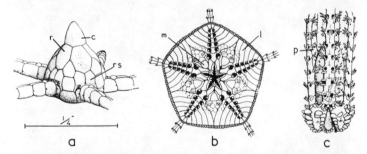

a   b   c

Fig. 17. Some bizarre brittle-stars. a) *Ophiopyrgus wyvillethomsoni*, in
oblique interradial view to show the high disc and conical central plate,
b) *Astrophiura marionae* in ventral view, showing the extension of the disc
by the proximal lateral arm plates and c) *Ophiotholia supplicans* in radial
side view. In all three the outer parts of the arms have been omitted; (*c*)
central and (*r*) radial plates, (*rs*) radial shield, (*l*) lateral arm plate, (*m*)
madreporite and (*p*) parasol-shaped hook. In the particular specimen of
Astrophiura shown, the oral shields, other than the madreporite, though
thin and transparent, are unusually distinct in outline; in most specimens
they are irregular and, together with the other superficial plates between
them and the edge of the extended disc, tend to form a delicate mosaic

been studied. *Ophiotholia* and certain related genera are also peculiar in having several small parasol- (or umbrella-) shaped hooks of unknown function on each of the more distal lateral arm plates. Returning to *Astrophiura*, this has an extraordinary extension of the proximal lateral arm plates into horizontal flanges, the consecutive ones fitting closely together and ending abruptly at about the same distance from the mouth; they have a fringe of short spinelets along their free edges. The result of this is to extend the disc into a pentagon probably about twice its original diameter. The narrow outer parts of the arms project abruptly from the corners of the extended disc. They resemble the corresponding parts of the arms of some other genera of the Ophiuridae, including *Ophiopygrus*, in having the lateral arm plates greatly enlarged and widely in contact to the exclusion of the dorsal and ventral plates. In *Ophiopyrgus* small dorsal and ventral plates only remain on the proximal arm segments, but the majority of brittle-stars have all four series of arm plates well developed throughout the arm length, though the shapes and sizes of these vary considerably in different species.

The lateral arm plates of Ophiurae each bear a vertical series of arm spines. Usually these form a divergent comb projecting at right angles to the axis of the arm, with the middle spines the longest and equal in length to about half the width of the segment. This is the most common condition in families like the Amphiuridae and the Ophiactidae, where certain species may also have one or more spines modified into a hook. The families Ophiotrichidae and Ophiacanthidae have the spines, particularly the more dorsal ones, very long and often thorny, their length sometimes considerably exceeding the width of the segment. In *Ophiopteron* and some juvenile specimens of *Ophiothrix* each series of spines is webbed by skin to form a fan. Conversely, most members of the families Ophiodermatidae and more particularly the Ophiuridae, have inconspicuous spines lying flat alongside the succeeding lateral arm plate and rarely even as long as the segment. In *Ophioderma* the spatulate spines are numerous, often 10 or 11 in each series, but in *Ophiura* and its relatives the spines are few, sometimes reduced to only one or two, as well as being small and peg-like in shape.

The relative arm length varies considerably in brittle-stars, from a minimum of about twice the disc diameter in some of the Ophiuridae to about twenty times in *Macrophiothrix longipeda* of the family Ophiotrichidae.

The most important characters by which the families of brittle-stars are distinguished are probably those provided by the papillae fringing the edges of the jaws and supplementing the vertical series of teeth placed at the apex of each jaw. Some examples of different jaw types are

Starfishes and related echinoderms

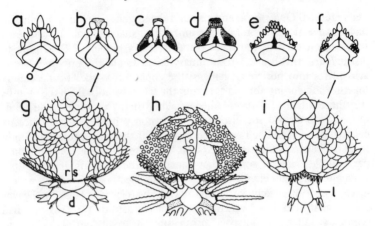

Fig. 18. Details of various brittle-stars. a) to f) single jaws of species of: a) *Ophiacantha*, b) *Amphipholis*, c) *Ophiactis*, d) *Ophiothrix*, e) *Ophiocomina* and f) *Ophiura*, for comparison with those of *Amphiura* in fig. 5c. In c) to f) the two pores for the oral tube feet or tentacles are visible but in a) and b) they are concealed behind the oral papillae; g) to i) dorsal view of part of the disc and one arm base of: g) *Amphipholis*, h) *Ophiothrix* and i) *Ophiura*. In h) the arm spines of the outer segment drawn are shown displaced for the sake of clarity; (*o*) oral shield, (*rs*) radial shields, (*d*) dorsal arm plate, (*l*) lateral arm plate

shown in fig. 18. The most distinctive are probably those of the Ophiotrichidae, where there is only a compact cluster of small blunt papillae at the apex, and those of the Amphiuridae, where there are two large rectangular apical papillae below the lowest tooth and one or more other papillae each side on the outer part of the jaw. The number and arrangement of these are characteristic of certain of the genera of Amphiurids; for instance *Amphipholis* has one wide and one narrow papilla each side of and in series with the apical pair. In the Ophiacanthidae the papillae are large and pointed, forming continuous series with one or several at the apex, while the Ophiuridae have smaller papillae and the Ophiodermatidae and Ophiocomidae have blunter ones, the latter also having a cluster at the apex.

Finally, the form of the disc covering also varies throughout the group and in many cases is characteristic of species, genera or even families. The scaling is usually distinct, particularly in the Amphiuridae, Ophiactidae and Ophiuridae. Sometimes it is obscured by thickening of the skin, or the scales themselves may be reduced. Otherwise, they may be more or less concealed by a covering of granules, as in *Ophiocoma* and *Ophioderma,* or by spinelets or thorny stumps as in the families Ophiotrichidae and Ophiacanthidae.

In the young brittle-star six primary plates are the first to be developed, one in the centre of the disc and five others situated in the radii around it. As the disc enlarges, further scales are nearly always formed around and usually between these primaries, which eventually become indistinguishable. However, in some species, especially of the family Amphiuridae and even more the Ophiuridae, the primary plates are still distinct in the adult. *Ophiopyrgus* (fig. 17a) has only a few other plates besides the primaries but the greatest reduction in number is shown by the genus *Ophiotypa* where the six primaries occupy the whole dorsal side of the disc to the exclusion of all other plates. Apart from the primaries, and regardless of their distinctness or otherwise, nearly all species of brittle-stars have a conspicuous pair of enlarged plates on the dorsal side of the disc opposite the base of each arm. These are the radial shields and their shape and size are often important in identification. Even when the disc is covered with granules or spinelets, as in most species of *Ophiothrix* and *Ophiacantha* for instance, these are usually reduced in size and number, if not absent altogether, on the radial shields.

As for size, the basket-stars particularly grow quite large, up to about ten cm. in disc diameter, while their total diameter with the arms fully extended may exceed 60 cm. Most of the Ophiurae are much smaller, averaging about ten mm. in disc diameter and from ten to twelve cm. arm span, although the tropical Indo-Pacific species *Ophiarachna incrassata* is known to reach a disc diameter of over five cm. This is a very handsome star; apart from its size, the colour is very striking, being a bright grass-green, with the disc decorated by white spots encircled by black rings. Other brittle-stars have a variety of colour and patterns, usually with a banded effect on the arms and often with the radial shields a contrasting colour. In some species the colour may be characteristic, but in others like the British *Ophiothrix fragilis* the range is so great that it is hard to find two specimens with identical patterns. Many of the shallow-water Ophiurida are marked with blues or purples. The reds and oranges so frequent in starfishes are less common, except among those Euryalida which live in association with reddish sea fans. Burrowing forms, such as most of the Amphiurids, as well as species like *Ophiura albida* that live on sand, are often simply grey in colour.

No pedicellariae are found in ophiuroids, though the parasol-shaped hooks on the distal arm segments of *Ophiotholia* have been likened to them.

71

Starfishes and related echinoderms

Sea-Urchins, Cake-Urchins and Heart-Urchins (Echinoidea)

Having lent itself in the formation of the name Echinodermata, the Greek word 'echinos' has also been applied to those spiniest of 'spiny-skins', the sea-urchins. This terminology, used by Aristotle, has been carried down into modern nomenclature by Linnaeus who, in 1758, included under the generic name *Echinus* all the species of echinoids known to him, both regular and irregular. However, the one which Aristotle probably knew best, because its roes have been used as food in Mediterranean countries since ancient times, was only formally described and named *Echinus lividus* by Lamarck in 1816. It is now placed in a separate genus called *Paracentrotus*.

At the present time (1977) nearly 800 species of living echinoids are recognized, of which 16 occur in British waters at depths of less than 100 fathoms (183 metres). These include several species of *Echinus* itself, notably the large *Echinus esculentus*, as well as heart-urchins like *Echinocardium cordatum*, but no large cake-urchins such as are found in North American and in warmer waters.

Owing to their compact body form and often stout skeleton, echinoids have made particularly good fossils and a large number of extinct groups are known. Those surviving to the present day are placed in as many as 48 families grouped into 15 orders. A number of these orders are super-ficially rather similar and can be further grouped under the popular terms sea-urchins, cake-urchins (or sand-dollars) and heart-urchins. The cake- and heart-urchins together are called irregular echinoids, since their tests are modified with some degree of bilateral symmetry in contrast to the regular echinoids or ordinary sea-urchins where the radial symmetry is almost perfect. Some regular sea-urchins are globular in shape, though the majority are more or less flattened, especially on the lower surface, so that the outline of the test is circular only in dorsal or ventral view. The mouth and anus are both placed centrally on the lower and upper surfaces, as if at the south and north poles respectively. The anus lies in the centre of the apical system, ringed by the five genital plates with their openings (fig. 5b). In the irregular echinoids the anus has moved from the apical area and lies instead in an interradius, either laterally, or even on the flattened lower surface (fig. 7). The interradius containing the anus is posterior and the radius opposite to it anterior, since these echinoids habitually move with the same radius in front. Simultaneously, the test has lost the globular form and is either considerably flattened in most of the cake-urchins, or else egg-shaped with the long axis antero-posterior in alignment in the heart-urchins.

The latter also have the mouth shifted forwards away from the centre of the lower side.

All the echinoids have the test made up of twenty vertical series of flattened, mostly hexagonal, plates, usually joined together rigidly at their edges. These are called coronal plates and the series are arranged in pairs, with five pairs of ambulacral plates bearing the tube feet alternating with five pairs of fewer, but larger, interambulacral plates. Each ray, corresponding to an arm of a starfish or brittle-star, is represented by two series of ambulacral plates, together with one series of interambulacrals on either side.

As in the starfishes, the tube feet of echinoids have internal bulbs or ampullae connected with the external cavity of each foot through pores in the ambulacral plates. In echinoids these pores are paired and each plate has one pair of pores corresponding to one foot. This is clearly shown in the primitive order Cidaroida, where the pore-pairs form vertical series one above the other (fig. 19a). In the other present-day regular echinoids, however, the tube feet and ambulacral plates are more numerous and the plates have become fused into groups of three or more. At the same time the pore-pairs of these compound plates are staggered in position and tend to form oblique or even nearly horizontal

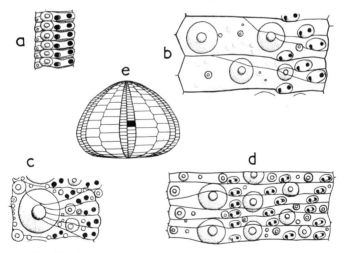

Fig. 19. Details of ambulacral plates of some regular echinoids. a) Six simple plates of a Cidarid, b) two compound plates of *Echinus*, c) one compound plate of *Echinometra* and d) six compound plates of *Trip-neustes*. [The dark patch in e) shows the approximate position from which the enlargements were taken]

arcs. In the tropical genus *Tripneustes* (fig. 19d) this displacement has resulted in three vertical lines of pore-pairs up each series of ambulacral plates and the already compound plates are integrated further; another tropical genus, *Echinometra*, has curved arcs of six or more pore-pairs.

The coronal plates bear a number of knobs or tubercles of different size and arrangement according to the species. On these the spines are mounted. Around the tubercle of each larger or primary spine is a convex zone called the areole, to which the muscles supporting and controlling the spine are attached. In the Cidaroida the primary spines and their accompanying areoles are particularly large. Moreover, when the spines are fully grown their skin covering wears off leaving them vulnerable to the settlement of organisms such as barnacles, tube worms and sponges. Some Cidarids may carry about quite a diverse community of these encrusting forms (Plate VIII, fig. a).

Another characteristic of the Cidaroida is that a ring of small, flattened, secondary spines surrounds the areole of each primary one, giving a very distinctive appearance to the test (Plate VIII, figs. a and c). Most of the non-cidarid species of regular echinoids have a more or less bristly covering of numerous tapering spines, the longest of them usually less than half the diameter of the test, often much shorter as in *Echinus* (Plate I, fig. d) and *Tripneustes*. Among the notable exceptions to this is *Heterocentrotus*, of which the huge primary spines have prompted the name of 'slate-pencil' urchin (Plate VIII, fig. g). Its secondary spines are short but very thick and form a dense covering to the test between the primaries. In a related genus called *Colobocentrotus* (Plate VIII, fig. e), also from the shallow waters of the Indian and west Pacific oceans, there are no long primary spines on the upper side; instead all the spines on that surface are similar, very short, thick and polygonal in cross section, so that their flat tips form a mosaic-like surface. On the flattened under side the spines are very reduced, and at the same time the tube feet are more numerous and crowded. Each compound ambulacral plate is formed of about twelve small plates with a corresponding number of pore-pairs forming a compact arc, the successive arcs being closely crowded together. Around the edge of the test, between upper and lower surfaces, is a fringe of large flattened spines like the petals of a daisy, projecting outwards and slightly downwards. All these specializations help *Colobocentrotus* to survive on rocky shores pounded by surf. The smooth upper surface gives the minimum resistance to the waves, and the numerous tube feet help it to cling on like a limpet under a force that would dislodge any ordinary sea-urchin. *Heterocentrotus* and *Colobocentrotus* belong to a family called the Echinometridae, named after *Echinometra*, another tropical

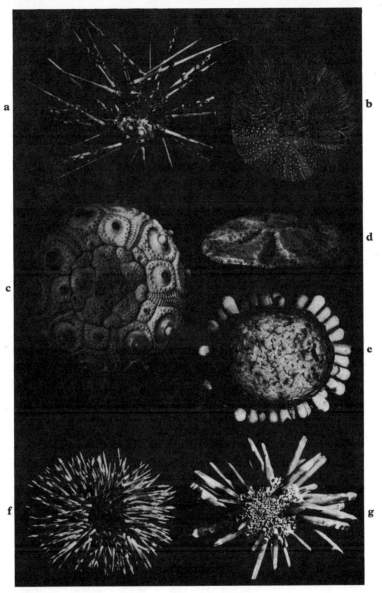

Plate VIII. Regular echinoids: a) *Histocidaris* with numerous barnacles growing on the long primary spines (after Mortensen); b) *Echinus esculentus* with some of the short spines removed; c) test of a Cidarid without spines, enlarged to show the various plates and the huge primary tubercles; d) oblique side view of a collapsed specimen of the Echinothuriid *Phormosoma*, showing the flexible test; e), f) and g) three tropical Echinometrids with elongated tests, e) *Colobocentrotus*, adapted for surf-beaten shores, f) *Echinometra* and g) *Heterocentrotus*. All are seen from above, except for d)

genus but one with less specialized, slender tapering spines (Plate VIII, fig. f). All three genera differ from the other regular sea-urchins in having the test oval in outline, when seen in dorsal or ventral view (fig. 6b).

Another regular echinoid remarkable for its spines is *Diadema* (Plate XV) a real menace of the tropical reefs. Its upper spines may be as much as 30 cm. in length, being much longer than the test is wide. They are very slender, hollow, sharp and brittle, so that they can impale any incautious animal that touches them and break off in the wound.

Hollow spines are also found in the aberrant family Echinothuriidae, where those of the ventral side may have a kind of hoof at the tip, or else a glandular sac, often containing poison. The Echinothuriids are remarkable for their flexible, leathery tests, the plates being embedded in skin, in contrast to nearly all the other regular sea-urchins where the test is rigid. The Echinothuriids are flattish, deep-sea forms; in life their upper sides are probably domed, but when brought up to the surface in a dredge they collapse owing to the change in pressure. As a result, preserved specimens usually resemble rather limp discs (Plate VIII, fig. d). Another difference, this time shared with the Cidarids, is that the flexible peristome, or area around the mouth, is covered with continuous series of plates, unlike most other sea-urchins where the skin of the peristome has few plates and those widely spaced. This is believed to be a primitive character.

Many Echinothuriids grow to a very large size, and the only recorded specimen of a Japanese species called *Sperosoma giganteum* is over 30 cm. in diameter, larger than any other echinoid.

Whilst the large British sea-urchin *Echinus esculentus* grows to a diameter of about 15 cm., most species are about 5–12 cm. across, and a few may never exceed 12 mm. The only cake-urchin found in British seas, *Echinocyamus pusillus*, is one of the smallest, the flattened oval test being usually about 5 mm. in length. Although *Echinocyamus* is common in areas of coarse sand or gravel, in fairly shallow water, it is so inconspicuous that few people notice it.

Most of the other cake-urchins, or sand dollars as they are called in America, are larger and flatter than *Echinocyamus*, and some are more nearly circular in outline. The centre of the upper surface is elevated in a few species, so that in profile they appear very slightly conical. The test is supported internally by a number of vertical pillars, and in certain genera, such as the key-hole urchin *Mellita*, there are also some symmetrically placed slits or lunules perforating right through it or cutting in at intervals around part of the margin. *Rotula*, another genus of a separate family, is distinguished by a series of horizontal lobes

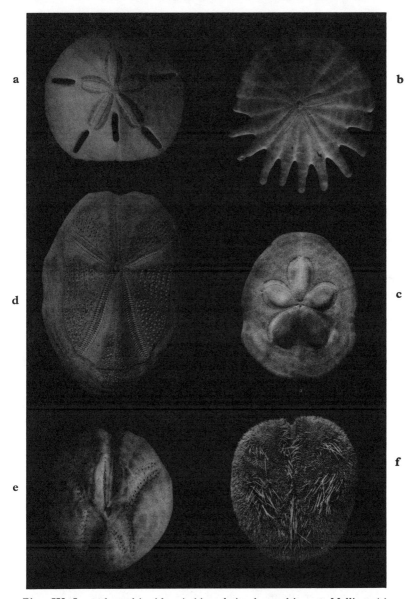

Plate IX. Irregular echinoids: a), b) and c) cake-urchins, a) *Mellita* with lunules in the test, b) *Rotula* with posterior prongs and c) *Clypeaster*, all with the fine spines removed to show the 'petals'; d), e) and f) heart-urchins, d) the large West Indian *Plagiobrissus* with a peripetalous fasciole and regularly placed primary tubercles, e) and f) British species of *Echinocardium* and *Spatangus*, the latter with the spines intact. All are viewed from the dorsal side

projecting around the posterior part of the test like a fringe (Plate IX, fig. b). Both these structural modifications must give added strength to the test, and probably help speed up burrowing. In some cake-urchins the posterior part is the more vulnerable, since it may be exposed above the surface of the sand or mud while the anterior end is buried.

In all the irregular echinoids now living, the anus is in a posterior position, but a few fossil species show transitional stages in its migration away from the centre of the apical system, the genital plates being modified in their positions and relative sizes. This shift must have been correlated with the tendency for the urchin to travel always with the same ambulacrum in front (designated III or D according to the different systems of orientation (p. 13)). The posterior position of the anus then becomes an advantage, as the waste products are left behind, instead of fouling up the area through which the urchin is about to move. The adoption of a burrowing habit and inclination of the spines backwards to reduce resistance are also linked with the development of bilateral symmetry in irregular echinoids.

A few genera surviving to the present day also show transitional stages in the development and arrangement of the ambulacral plates and pores. In *Echinoneus* the condition is much as in the regular echinoids, with continuous series of pores from apical system to peristome, although the test is ovate and the anus posterior and ventral. However, nearly all the other irregular species have a reduction of the pores in the ambital region (that is at the widest part of the test) and the outermost ones of each double ambulacral series on the upper surface tend to converge towards each other near the ambitus, producing a petal-like shape. The five 'petals' radiating out from the apical area give a very attractive flower-like effect on denuded tests of both cake- and heart-urchins (Plate IX, figs. a to e).

The heart-urchins represent the greatest deviation from the radially symmetrical form among echinoids, since not only is the anus shifted posteriorly but the mouth lies anteriorly, sometimes almost at the extreme front end. At the same time the teeth have been lost, together with the complex internal apparatus for operating them which is found in regular echinoids (and in a modified form in cake-urchins). The test is usually more or less ovate, much higher than in the cake-urchins and with the ambitus rounded, there being no sharp margin. The anterior or frontal ambulacrum may be rather sunken, so that the whole animal becomes heart-shaped in dorsal view. This is very distinct in *Spatangus* itself as well as in *Echinocardium*, both genera including common British species (Plate IX, figs. e and f).

In irregular echinoids most of the spines do not stand erect, but are inclined backwards. They are usually very fine, small and numerous and in cake-urchins particularly, resemble a coat of short fur. In the heart-urchins the spines of the lower surface are enlarged, with curved, spade-like tips, being especially modified for burrowing forwards through sand; some primary spines on the upper side may be more or less enlarged, rather like the bristles of a porcupine, in genera such as *Plagiobrissus* and *Spatangus*. The spines are not always uniform or evenly graduated over the whole test but may leave some areas, particularly on the lower side, more or less naked.

Another feature that contributes to the symmetrical patterns found on the tests of heart-urchins when the spines are removed, is the presence of narrow bands called fascioles. These are differentiated from the rest of the surface by the concentration in them of numerous minute tubercles, in life bearing special ciliated spinelets. The fascioles describe loops on the test in various positions according to the genera, and their exact shape may vary in different species. The most common type found is the subanal, a loop below the anus. This is the only kind of fasciole in the genus *Spatangus*, but *Echinocardium* has both subanal and inner fascioles, the latter circumscribing the anterior petal. *Protenaster*, shown in fig. 7b, has a peripetalous fasciole (circumscribing all the petals) continued backwards as a lateral fasciole. Usually only one or two types occur in any one genus. Their function is to produce water currents.

Other superficial structures of value in classifying echinoids, but this time present throughout the group, are the pedicellariae. As in the starfishes, these are minute pincer-like organs, barely visible with the naked eye, especially adapted for grasping. However, in the echinoids they are always highly specialized, no forms transitional with spinelets being found in any member of the class. They also differ from the pincer-like pedicellariae of the forcipulate starfishes in having usually three valves, rarely two or four, as well as in being individually mounted on long, movable stalks.

Pedicellariae may arise from nearly all parts of the surface of an echinoid. The regular sea-urchins related to *Echinus* have four distinct basic types, each with a particular function. Those of a single type may therefore be concentrated on a certain area, for instance on the peristome around the mouth. The frequency of occurrence and the exact form of the valves vary from one species to another and often one or more types of pedicellaria may be absent altogether, notably in the Cidarids which have only two of them.

The most specialized type of pedicellaria is the globiferous, several of which are shown in fig. 20. These are defensive in function and each

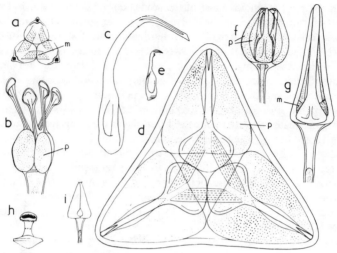

Fig. 20. Pedicellariae of various echinoids. a) Globiferous one of the Cidarid *Rhopalocidaris*, open and viewed from above, b) dactylous of the Echinothuriid *Araeosoma*, with spoon-shaped tips to the four (or five) valves, in side view, c) single valve in side view and d) whole globiferous pedicellaria of *Toxopneustes*, open and viewed from above, e) single valve and f) whole globiferous of *Echinus*, both in side view, g) tridentate of *Echinus* in side view, h) single valve of ophicephalous of the cake-urchin *Clypeaster*, viewed from the inner face and i) bidentate (i.e. two-valved) of another cake-urchin, *Echinarachnius*; (*m*) adductor muscles and (*p*) poison sacs. [Magnifications: a) to g) ×50, h) and i) ×100.] (After Mortensen)

valve has a poison gland associated with it, giving the pedicellaria as a whole a bulbous appearance when closed. The tip of the valve is usually modified into a large, incurved fang, sometimes with smaller teeth at each side of it. These pedicellariae are kept gaping open when at rest, but the touch of a foreign body stimulates their adductor muscles to snap them shut, the fangs making a puncture and the poison sacs contracting to inject their secretion along a channel in each fang. The globiferous pedicellariae of Cidarids (fig. 20a) have a poison-secreting cavity within each valve and no external sacs. The large size of the globiferous pedicellariae in the genus *Toxopneustes*, compared with those of most regular echinoids, can be seen from the figure; when opened they measure nearly five mm. between the tips of the valves. Conversely, most of the cake-urchins and heart-urchins have very small pedicellariae, the two shown in the figure being enlarged twice as much as those of the regular species. It is particularly among the cake-urchins that numbers of valves other than three are found, some species having bidentate pedicellariae with two valves (fig. 20i), while others have four or even five valves.

Another structure, the form of which has value in classification, is the chewing apparatus or Aristotle's lantern, present in the regular sea-urchins and, in a modified form, in the cake-urchins too. It consists of a framework of skeletal bars supporting the five large vertically aligned teeth, together with powerful muscles to operate the teeth (Plate XIII, fig. b).

Finally, the colour of echinoids covers an immense range; possibly greens and browns predominate but some are red, purple or black, or else so pale as to be nearly white. The spines and the skin covering the test are usually similar in colour but may contrast with each other, as in *Echinometra* (Plate VIII, fig. f), or the spines may be banded or tipped with another colour. When skin and spines are removed, the denuded test is usually different again, often beautifully shaded, and with the spine tubercles showing as pearly white knobs.

A few species are capable of a slow change in shade according to the light intensity, by expansion or contraction of pigment areas in the skin called chromatophores. This has been noted particularly in the tropical *Diadema*, which is also remarkable for the difference in colour of the young and the adult, the early black and white banded effect (Plate XV) changing to all black (or purple) as growth proceeds.

Sea-Cucumbers (Holothurioidea)

The Greeks are once again responsible for the name now used for this class. However, it is not certain that Aristotle's 'Holothuria' was the same kind of animal as the one we know by that name, since he compared it with the oyster, noting that both are unattached but immobile.

Linnaeus, in the tenth edition of his *Systema Naturae* published in 1758, ignored Aristotle's usage and gave the name *Holothuria* to certain free-swimming animals such as the Portuguese man-of-war, a Coelenterate related to the jellyfishes. Later, in his enlarged 1767 edition, Linnaeus did introduce some sea-cucumber species into the genus. Then in 1801, the Portuguese man-of-war was renamed *Physalia*, after the specific name *physalis* used by Linnaeus. This became generally adopted and *Holothuria* was left to cover the bottom-living sea-cucumbers.

Linnaeus was the pioneer of the present system of binomial or two-name nomenclature for animals (that is designation by a generic and a specific name). When the International Commission for Zoological Nomenclature was set up in 1895 to try and bring order and conformity to the naming of animals, it took the date of his tenth edition of the *Systema Naturae* (1758) as the starting point for the recognition of scientific names. All names of earlier date were then rejected, unless they were repeated subsequently by zoologists conforming to Linnaeus' two-name system. By the rules of the Commission, the name *Holothuria* should have been used for *Physalia* and another name altogether found for the sea-cucumbers. To avoid such an undesirable upset in long established usage, a special exception to the rules was made to date *Holothuria* only back as far as 1767 and to ignore those species then included in it by Linnaeus which were not sea-cucumbers. It was unfortunate that Linnaeus did not recognize instead the genus *Cucumis*, also used by Aristotle, but for an undoubted sea-cucumber. It has since been revived in the modified form of *Cucumaria*, but only gives its name to a family, the Cucumariidae, not to the entire class as *Holothuria* has done.

Over 900 species of holothurians are generally accepted, but, since some of the characters used in their identification need special techniques to show them up, it is likely that certain of the names given to species, particularly those described before 1900 and not since recognized, may prove to be synonyms of others better known.

As many as twenty-one species have been recorded from British waters at depths of less than 100 fathoms (183 metres), which is a greater proportion of the total than for any other class of Echinoderms. One of the most conspicuous is the large fleshy *Cucumaria frondosa*, living around the Scottish coasts at low tide mark and beyond. Adults of *C. frondosa* reach a length of about 40 cm. Because of their dark colour and sausage-like shape, some fishermen call them 'puddings'. Another holothurian found in western Scotland and on English coasts as well is the 'cotton-spinner', *Holothuria forskali* (named after an early Danish biologist). The popular name is derived from its defensive habit of ejecting masses of sticky white threads to distract or even entangle any attacker. The other holothurians found in our waters are smaller and mostly less common, though the small, worm-like *Leptosynapta* is numerous, particularly on the west coast.

In form the majority of holothurians are elongated like a small cucumber or sausage, with the five ambulacra running along the length of the body. At one end is the mouth surrounded by a ring of tentacles and at the other is the anus. Since the end with the mouth habitually leads the way when these animals move about, it can be called anterior and the end with the anus posterior.

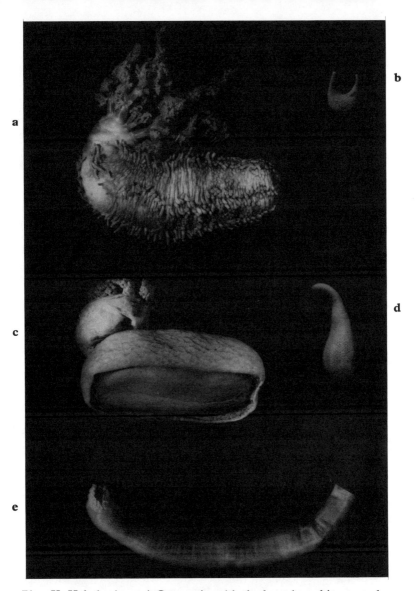

Plate X. Holothurians: a) *Cucumaria*, with the large branching tentacles extended (the anterior end is bent backwards in this preserved specimen), b) the diminutive, U-shaped *Echinocucumis*, c) *Psolus*, viewed obliquely from below to show the specialized sole (the anterior end is unnaturally distorted), d) *Rhopalodina*, with mouth and anus both opening at the tip of the vertical 'probiscis' and e) the front half of the worm-like *Leptosynapta*

Starfishes and related echinoderms

The class Holothurioidea is generally divided into five orders distinguished primarily by differences in the tentacles and in the tube feet. Of the two largest orders, the Aspidochirotida, including *Holothuria*, have small, leaf-shaped tentacles, the short stalk of each ending in many branches radiating in a single plane, while the other big group, the Dendrochirotida, like *Cucumaria*, is characterized by larger, irregularly branching and rather bush-like tentacles. Species of the order Apodida have simpler tentacles with a series of lobes or digits branching off on each side of a central stalk. In the British *Labidoplax digitata*, the stalk is abbreviated and there are only four finger-like lobes. This form is called digitate. However, as in *Synaptula* (fig. 21c) and *Leptosynapta* for instance, the stalk may be elongated and have paired digits along its length, making a pinnate type of tentacle. The Molpadida and a few of the deep-sea Elasipodida also have digitate tentacles, usually with very short digits, but most Elasipodids have simplified leaf-shaped ones rather like those of the Aspidochirotids.

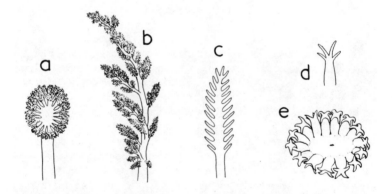

Fig. 21. Various kinds of holothurian tentacles. a) Leaf-shaped of the Aspidochirotid *Actinopyga* (related to *Holothuria*) [after Hyman]. b) bush-shaped of the Dendrochirotid *Cucumaria*, c) pinnate of the Apodid *Synaptula* [after Oersted], d) digitate of the Apodid *Labidoplax* [after Cuénot] and e) complete ring of digitate tentacles of the Molpadid *Caudina* [after Gerould]

The number of tentacles is usually 10 or 20, or other multiples of five, but most numbers between 8 and 30 have been recorded. Since they are delicate and vulnerable compared to the thickened body wall, many holothurians can retract their tentacles out of sight within a fold of the wall immediately behind them. In the Dendrochirotids with their big tentacles, the body wall itself is thin and pliable for some distance behind the tentacles and powerful internal retractor muscles are developed to pull the entire front end, or introvert, of the animal partly inside out within the body cavity.

Most Dendrochirotids are also peculiar in having some of the tentacles much smaller than the rest. In *Cucumaria*, where there are 10 tentacles, the two ventral-most of these are very reduced (fig. 8a), while *Phyllophorus*, with 20 tentacles arranged in two concentric rings of fifteen and five, has all five inner ones small as well as some of the outer series.

Inside the body cavity and encircling the gut close behind the mouth is a collar of plates called the calcareous ring. This is associated with the water ring canal which similarly encircles the gut, as in other Echinoderms. From this ring lead five radial canals to run down the ambulacra to the tube feet and their ampullae after giving off branches to the tentacles. In many holothurians there are also ampullae associated with the tentacles. The presence of these connections with the water vascular system indicates that, during the evolution of the holothurians, the tentacles have been developed from those tube feet nearest the mouth.

The ordinary tube feet still have their primitive arrangement in two rows along each radius or ambulacrum in some species, notably of the family Cucumariidae. However, in many others the feet have become scattered over the whole surface and the radii are hardly distinct externally. Most holothurians habitually lie, either exposed on the seabed or burrowed into it, in such a way that the same side is always downwards. Three of the radii or ambulacra thus run along the lower side, which can be termed ventral, while the other two are dorsal. In comparison with the orientation of the other Echinoderm classes (see p. 17), the mid-ventral radius can be designated as A, since the single water pore or madreporite, when present, lies in the mid-dorsal interradius, prompting its designation as CD. The genital opening is single in holothurians, unlike the other classes, and also opens in this mid-dorsal interradius.

In many species of *Holothuria* itself the body is slightly flattened dorso-ventrally, while the tube feet of the dorsal side are simplified or reduced in number and size, often losing the terminal sucking disc and having their internal ampullae reduced. Some of them may even be modified into large warts. The ventral tube feet, on the contrary, usually have an important locomotory function and are often very numerous and prominent. This is true of most Aspidochirotids (*Holothuria* and its relatives) but not of such Dendrochirotids as *Cucumaria*, the species of which are much less active. Many Dendrochirotids, in fact, have the tube feet not only reduced in number but rendered incapable of retracting owing to stiffening with many crowded calcareous spicules.

As the name suggests, the species of the order Apodida have no tube feet. Most are burrowing forms, but some, like the large tropical species *Synapta maculata*, crawl about exposed on the sea-bed, particularly in sandy parts of coral reefs. All of them, whatever their habits, have very little dorso-ventral specialization in comparison with most other holothurians.

Among the Dendrochirotids, the dorso-ventral specialization does not involve flattening, but instead the whole body, seen in side view, is more or less U-shaped, with the front and hind ends pointed upwards. This is an advantage for burrowing forms as their main apertures can be kept clear. Some burrowing Molpadids also have a 'tail' that curves upwards. The small Dendrochirotid *Echinocucumis* (Plate X, fig. b) has an almost spherical body with the two conical ends standing up from it. The limit of dorsal displacement of mouth and anus is reached by *Rhopalodina* (Plate X, fig. d). This has a bulbous body with the mouth and anus both opening at the tip of a single long, stalk-like extension standing up vertically from it, often three or four times as long as the body itself.

Members of another Dendrochirotid family, the Psolidae, also have a specialized and peculiar form. The genus *Psolus* is rather slug-like, since its ventral side is modified into a distinct sole for creeping and clinging on to hard surfaces. At the same time, the tube feet are restricted to the three ventral radii, particularly the lateral ones (B and E). Again the two extremities are deflected dorsally.

The order Elasipodida includes many species of extraordinary form specially modified for life in very deep water. In fact Elasipodids are among the very few animals trawled up from the abyssal trenches of the oceans (though the depth record of over 5,500 fathoms for an Echinoderm is held by an insignificant member of the Apodida). Like the Psolids, many Elasipodids have the locomotory tube feet restricted, in this case either to single rows in radii B and E or to a double row in the mid-ventral radius A. In most Elasipodids the dorso-ventral modification of the body is well marked. The mouth is usually displaced on to the ventral side, following a tendency shown also in the Aspido-chirotida in contrast to the Dendrochirotida. Other modifications in some of these deep-sea holothurians include the development of lateral flanges or fins, large paired dorsal processes, more rarely a median dorsal crest or sometimes a tail-like projection. These devices probably assist in stabilizing or buoying up the body or even in propelling it through the water, since it is believed that many Elasipodids can swim. Specimens

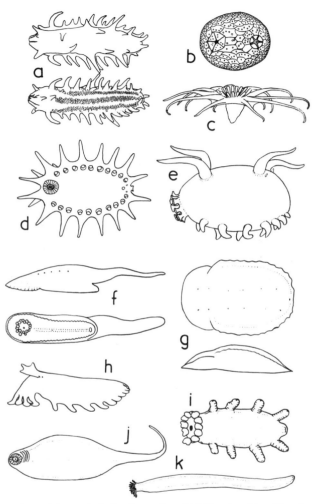

Fig. 22. Some bizarre holothurians. a) and b) Dendrochirotida, c) to f), h) and i) Elasipodida, g) Aspidochirotida, j) Molpadida and k) Apodida. a) *Colochirus quadrangularis* in dorsal and ventral views, the tentacles retracted, b) *Psolus diomediae* in dorsal view, retracted [after Ludwig], c) artist's impression of *Pelagothuria natatrix* in side view [after Chun], d) *Deima validum* in ventral view [after Théel], e) *Scotoplanes globosa* in side view [after Théel], f) *Psychropotes longicauda* in side and ventral views [after Théel], g) *Galatheathuria aspera* in dorsal and side views [after Hansen and Madsen], h) *Peniagone vedeli* in side view [after Hansen], i) *Elpidia glacialis* in ventral view [after Djakonov], j) *Molpadia musculus* in ventral view with the 'head' bent towards the observer [after H. L. Clark] and k) *Anapta gracilis*

of the aberrant genus *Pelagothuria* (fig. 22c) have even been found near the surface and may be quite independent of the sea bottom.

There are also a few deep-sea Aspidochirotids that have similarly become modified towards a free-swimming or pelagic life. Such a one is *Galatheathuria aspera* (fig. 22g) an oval, flattened holothurian with a distinct head and the rest of the body bearing a projecting rim around the edge.

The Elasipodids are unusual in having very few calcareous spicules in the skin so that they appear semi-transparent, though the body wall is often thickened and rather jelly-like.

The species of the order Apodida also tend to have relatively few spicules and to be rather transparent, but their body walls are very thin. Some of them have many small skin papillae crowded with little plates; in *Chiridota* for instance, these plates have the form of wheels (fig. 3i). Specimens of the large tropical genus *Synapta* may reach several feet in length, and their skin is more opaque and pigmented, though still thin. *Synapta* and its relatives are oddly sticky to the touch, due to projections of the anchor-shaped spicules in their skins. Each anchor has the tips of the two flukes curved not only backwards but slightly upwards from the horizontal plane of the shank. At the base of the shank the anchor is jointed to a flat oval anchor plate from which it normally stands out a little so that the flukes are parallel with the surface of the skin. Under pressure from above, or lateral tension by contraction of the skin, the shank is pushed down flat on to the plate and the tips of the flukes stand out far enough to roughen the surface. This gives the skin a grip on the substrate (or anything else with which it comes in contact) and allows the Synaptid to crawl by muscular contraction and relaxation without slipping back.

The exact form of the anchors and their plates differs in the various genera of the family Synaptidae and is usually characteristic. Similarly, in other families of holothurians, the skin spicules are often characteristic and may provide one of the most reliable means of distinguishing one species from another. As in the Synaptids, part of their function is to give roughness to the surface. Accordingly, each species usually has one kind of spicule with a set of spines or other projections standing out from a flat basal part. Different spicules, smoother in shape, are found deeper in the body wall, giving it strength and firmness but still allowing considerable expansion or contraction by sliding freely over one another. In *Holothuria* the two kinds of spicules are called 'tables' and, 'buttons' (figs. 3 c and d) but some relatives of *Cucumaria* have 'baskets' instead of 'tables', and 'buttons' which are often knobbly (fig. 3f). Most kinds of spicules are pierced with a number of holes since each one develops from the branching and fusion of the tips of a minute rod of calcium carbonate deposited by special cells in the skin. (The skeletal plates of other Echinoderms also form by a similar method, but their magnitude is so much greater that they soon appear opaque owing to the multiplicity of the layers of perforations.) In the tube feet of many holothurians there are usually supporting rods, sometimes with branched or perforated ends, while at the tip of each locomotor tube foot there is often a circular, sieve-like plate, bracing the disc.

Although in most holothurians all these spicules are too small, as well as too deep in the body wall, to be seen by the naked eye, there are a few species in which they are sufficiently prominent for this to be possible. This is the case in some species of the genus *Psolus*, like the north European *Psolus squamatus* and the Pacific species *diomediae* shown in fig. 22b. Here the spicules of the upper surface have become greatly enlarged to form overlapping scales, completely armouring the whole exposed surface of the holothurian above the basal sole. In *P. diomediae* five scales around the opening for the retractable introvert, and five others around the anus, are modified into valves to protect these vulnerable parts. Some other Dendrochirotida apart from *Psolus* also have plates distinguishable with the naked eye, but elsewhere such enlargement is rare, or is limited to valves or knobs around the main openings.

The colours of live holothurians are mainly dull, with greys, browns, black or purple predominating. Most species are fairly uniform in colour all over, or else have a lighter shade on the underside, such as white, cream or pink, but some are patterned with light and dark markings. Pink and violet are common in the smaller burrowing species of the Apoda, but the larger ones with more opaque skins are often grey or brown. A few species of Dendrochirotida are bright red, orange or terra cotta, but these colours, so frequent in other Echinoderms, are uncommon among holothurians.

Sea-Lilies and Feather-Stars (Crinoidea)

There are two distinct kinds of present-day Crinoids, the sea-lilies with stalks and the feather-stars without. Although the stalked ones are probably better known as representative crinoids, they make up only a small proportion of the total number of living species, having had their heyday long ago in the Palaeozoic Era.

The name Crinoidea means 'lily-like' in Greek and refers of course to the stalked forms, superficially so plant-like. The suffix '-*crinus*' has commonly been used in sea-lily names such as *Metacrinus*, as well as for a few feather-stars like *Promachocrinus*. For a long time the close affinity between the two groups was not appreciated, partly because until 1755 sea-lilies were only known as fossils or as isolated, unrecognizable, fragments. In that year a specimen from deep-water off Martinique in the West Indies was shown to the French Academy, though its detailed description under the name of 'Palma marina' was not published until 1761. Soon afterwards a similar specimen from Barbados was demonstrated to the Royal Society in London. For the next half century and more, only a handful of specimens reached collectors in Europe and all of them came from the West Indian area. As late as 1835 a French dictionary included a misleading reproduction of an earlier sea-lily drawing, showing the crinoid superimposed on a sea-shore background. This certainly heightened the illusion of a marine palm. About the same time, however, a real step forward was made by Dr. J. Vaughan Thompson. He had discovered what he took to be a minute sea-lily in shallow water off the coast of Ireland, describing this in 1827 under the name of *Pentacrinus europeus*. His further investigations, published in 1836, revealed the interesting fact that this miniature sea-lily was really only the young stage of a common European feather-star and not a species in its own right. This stalked larval stage is now called a pentacrinoid. The growing idea among zoologists that sea-lilies and feather-stars are closely related, was confirmed by this discovery.

For more than a hundred years after the first description no genuine sea-lily was found outside the West Indian area until in 1864 a species of quite a different kind, only known before as fossils, was dredged up from deep water off the Norwegian coast. Four years later it was fully described under the name of *Rhizocrinus lofotensis*. This discovery was comparable in impact on the scientific world to that of the living coelacanth in recent years and helped to stimulate further deep-sea dredging expeditions, notably the circumnavigation of the famous 'Challenger' between 1873 and 1876. As a result, enormous numbers of new species of deep-sea, as well as shallow-water, animals were brought to light, including some new sea-lilies.

At the present time (1977) only about 75 species of living stalked crinoids are recognized. There are no reliable records of their occurrence in shallow water but a few have been found at depths of a little less than 100 fathoms. However, nearly half of all those known extend into the depths beyond the 2,000 fathom mark and one species even to 4,500 fathoms (8,230 metres).

On the other hand the feather-stars are predominantly creatures of relatively shallow water and have been known to zoologists for a much longer time. The Mediterranean species of *Antedon* was mentioned by Columna in 1592 and the British one we now call *Antedon bifida* by

Plate XI. Crinoids: a) a tropical Comasterid with no cirri on the flat pentagonal centrodorsal and with up to eighteen arms arising from each radial plate by repeated branching, b) the antarctic stalked crinoid *Ptilocrinus* with no cirri on the (broken) stalk and five unbranched arms, c) enlargement of the pentacrinoid stage of the antarctic feather-star *Isometra*, the cirri just appearing on the centrodorsal or top joint of the stalk below which it will shortly break, d) the squat stalked crinoid *Holopus* from the West Indies, e) and f) the central part of *Antedon bifida* viewed from below e) showing the cirri arising from the centrodorsal and from above f) showing the central mouth with the anus to the left and the ambulacral grooves zig-zagging along the arms giving off branches to the pinnules

Lloyd[1] in 1699. Linnaeus listed two species in 1758, but included them in the genus *Asterias* together with the starfishes and brittle-stars. About 540 species of feather-stars are now known, though only two of these occur in British waters at depths of less than 100 fathoms (183 metres), *Antedon bifida*, which is locally common off western England and around the coast of Scotland and *Leptometra celtica* which is found in the Irish Sea at depths of 25 fathoms or more. The stalked *Rhizocrinus* is not known to extend within this depth range in British waters.

As for the body form of crinoids, the skeleton is by far the most conspicuous and solid of any Echinoderm, the plates being clearly visible through the thin skin over most of the surface. The skeletal structure in all the living species, both stalked and free, is rather similar. In the centre is a cup or calyx made up of two superimposed rings of plates, five basals and five radials. The radials are uppermost and alternate with the basals. Both series are prominent in the larval crinoid (fig. 9) which also shows a third ring of five plates—the orals—corresponding in alignment to the basals, but nearly always lost in the adult. The calyx is mounted either on the top of a jointed stalk or on a single plate modified from the top of the larval stalk and called the centrodorsal (despite its position on the side of the body that is undermost in life). Each radial plate may bear a single arm, but usually there are one or more forks near the base. Two genera, *Promachocrinus* and *Thaumatocrinus*, are exceptional in having ten radials in the adult rather than five, the extra ones growing up interradially between the five original ones. *Thaumatocrinus* has ten undivided arms but in *Promachocrinus* there is a fork at the second segment after each radial so that the arms number twenty.

In most species of feather-stars the plates of the calyx are relatively reduced during development and the basals at least are not visible externally after the pentacrinoid stage. They can still be seen in a few primitive genera, much as in the majority of stalked forms.

In sea-lilies, the stalk has developed various devices for attachment to the sea-bed. This may involve a modification of the terminal plate with a disc or hold-fast or else the development of off-shoots from the stalk itself. These take two forms, being either irregular, branching, root-like processes from some of the lower stalk joints only, as in *Rhizocrinus*, or else unbranched, jointed cirri arising in groups at regular intervals up the stalk, as in *Metacrinus*. These cirri tend to curl downwards at the clawed tip so that they can grasp any convenient projection. Probably most of these forms with cirri on the stalk break adrift from

---

[1] This is the Lloyd whose name, in its Latin form, is perpetuated in the starfish *Luidia*.

their original basal attachments and can change their position to some extent by shifting the grip of the various cirri. In the stalk-less feather-stars cirri of similar type arising from the centrodorsal are nearly always present. The centrodorsal itself varies in shape in the different species, from flat and pentagonal to projecting and discoidal, hemispherical, conical or columnar. The shape of the plate, as well as the arrangement of the sockets for the cirri around it, may be characteristic in certain of the major groups.

 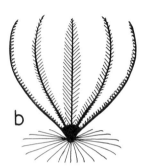

Fig. 23. Silhouettes of two feather-stars to show different proportions and forms of the attaching cirri. a) The ten-armed *Antedon bifida*, with short, stout, curved cirri and b) the five-armed *Pentametrocrinus varians*, with long, thin, straight ones

The characters provided by the cirri, that is their number, proportions, shape and the number of their segments, are also frequently used in classification. This is because one species differs considerably from another according to the type of surface favoured for settlement by the young. *Antedon bifida* for example has short, stout, rather strongly curved cirri suitable for gripping rocks or branching growths such as hydroids. *Leptometra celtica*, on the other hand, lives on soft, muddy surfaces and has the cirri long, slender and nearly straight so that they can cover the greatest possible area and provide a good anchorage. Even within a single genus the various species may show conspicuous differences in the relative proportions of the cirri, should they occupy different habitats. Some East Indian species such as *Comatula rotalaria*, usually found on loose coral sand, lose the cirri altogether in the adult, while the centrodorsal is reduced to a flat pentagon lying flush with the radials.

The arms of crinoids, like the cirri, are made up of a series of short, almost cylindrical segments jointed together to allow movement up and down more than from side to side. The arm segments are usually much thicker than those of the cirri and most of their joints have strong muscles. These muscular joints are oblique with respect to the long axis of the arm, and the consecutive ones alternate in alignment so that an almost zig-zag appearance results (Plate XI, figs. a and e). The regularity of this is upset at intervals by the presence of isolated non-muscular joints which show as a thin line absolutely transverse to the long axis. These ligamentous joints are called syzygies. They often occur between the third and fourth segments of each arm and at intervals of several ordinary joints beyond; sea-lilies may also have ligamentous joints in the stalk. The function of syzygies seems to be to act as emergency breaking points, so that part of the arm can be discarded, for instance should it be damaged or held fast by a predator.

Both among sea-lilies and feather-stars there are genera with five unbranched arms like the stalked *Rhizocrinus* and *Ptilocrinus* (Plate XI, fig. b) and the unstalked *Pentametrocrinus* (fig. 24e). However, in the vast majority, the second segment after each radial is an axillary one, that is it bears two separate branches on its outer side. Often too, the second or fourth (rarely the third) segment after this is another axillary. The series of plates leading up to and including each axillary are called division series. By the development of several consecutive division series the total number of arms may be as great as 200, though about forty is most common in the multibrachiate species (that is those with more than ten arms). The branching may be regular, each axillary having a corresponding one alongside it (fig. 24b) but often the subsequent divisions tend to be irregular or alternating, thereby avoiding over-crowding near the base. The stalked genus *Metacrinus* is exceptional in having long and irregular division series, mostly of more than four plates each (fig. 24c), unlike the feather-stars where two to four is the normal number.

The feathery appearance of crinoid arms is due to the series of thin jointed pinnules fringing the two sides of each arm. During development, each arm segment, except for the one following each axillary and the one preceding each syzygial joint, buds off a pinnule to one side or the other so that the consecutive ones are on opposite sides. Most of the pinnules are similar in size but a few at the base of each arm may be distinct. These are called oral pinnules. Sometimes they are very long, curl inwards at the tip and probably function as tactile organs in connection with the feeding. However, in certain species they are spike-like and project outwards and upwards, probably having a defensive function. Several pairs of pinnules following these oral ones each carry a sac-like genital organ. At the same time, like the outer pinnules but

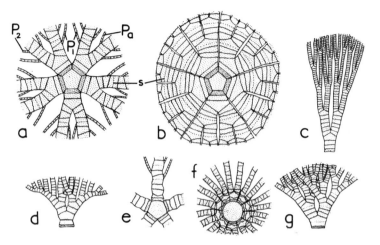

Fig. 24. Diagrams to show arm branching in various crinoids. a) *Antedon*-like form with ten arms (the bases of the first three pinnules of each arm are also shown); (*s*) syzygies, b) centre of a regular *Comanthus* with forty arms, the IIBr and IIIBr series all consisting of four plates, c) one ray of the stalked *Metacrinus*, with long and irregular division series, d) one ray of *Comatella nigra* with asymmetrical branching, all the division series having only two plates; the outermost series on the left is a VIBr, e) *Pentametrocrinus tuberculatus* with five arms; the first syzygy is between brachials 4 and 5; the pinnules on brachials 2 and 3 (i.e. P_1 and P_a) found in the related species *P. varians* are absent here, so the first pinnule, on brachial 5, is P_2, f) *Promachocrinus kerguelensis* with twenty arms, g) one ray of *Zygometra microdiscus* with irregular branching. The cirri have been omitted throughout for the sake of clarity and the radials are distinguished by heavier stippling [Mostly after A. H. Clark]

unlike the oral ones, these intermediate pinnules have a food groove along the upper surface leading to the main ambulacral groove of the arm, so that their purpose is twofold. The outer pinnules retain what is probably the primary function of these organs, namely that of gathering food. Together the pinnules cover a very considerable surface area, forming a comprehensive net to extract any edible microscopic matter from the surrounding water.

As with the cirri, the varying form of the pinnules, particularly the oral ones, provides many features characteristic of the species. In one family, the Comasteridae, the oral pinnules are very peculiar with many short, laterally compressed, segments, so that the outer part can coil up around any foreign body. Each of the outer segments has a knob or prong on the upper side, giving the end of the pinnule a saw-toothed appearance in profile. This is clearly a modification for grasping or even cutting up small objects, but unfortunately little has been done yet by way of observation on how live crinoids use their pinnules.

In scientific descriptions of crinoids, a number of abbreviations and symbols may be used, notably for the sequence of arm segments (brachials) and for the pinnules. The first division series following the radials, that is the plates up to and including the first axillary, are called the IBr series, the first plate being the IBr_1 and the second (usually the axillary itself) the IBr_2. When further division series occur these are called IIBr, IIIBr and so on. The brachials of the undivided arms are designated Br_1, Br_2, etc. As for the pinnules, those on the outer side of each arm, that is the side away from the corresponding arm of the pair (see fig. 24a) are numbered consecutively, while the alternating ones on the inner side are lettered. Br_1 rarely has a pinnule since it immediately follows an axillary so the first pinnule is nearly always found on the outer side of Br_2 and is called P_1. In many species Br_3 and Br_4 together make the first syzygial pair, shows as $3+4$. Br_3 therefore has no pinnule but Br_4 has one (P_a) on its inner side. The next pinnule, on the outer side of Br_5, is P_2, that on Br_6 P_b and so on.

With all these massive skeletal plates, the soft parts of crinoids are inconspicuous. Apart from the relatively small disc in the centre, containing the digestive tract, they are limited to a small cavity within the centrodorsal and radial ring, the ambulacral canals and grooves with their associated structures along the upper surfaces of the arms and pinnules, the muscles and ligaments linking the various segments together, a slender core of mainly nervous tissue through the centres of the brachials, pinnule and cirrus segments, as well as through the columnals when a stalk is present and finally the gonads along the genital pinnules. When the arms are more than five in number, the ambulacral groove of each one fuses with the others of the same radius near the edge of the disc and the five grooves so formed meet around the mouth, which is usually near the centre. In the crinoids the anus is on the upper surface like the mouth, but it opens at the tip of a cone or tube so that its discharge is carried clear of the food current leading to the mouth (fig. 5d).

Apart from their oral pinnules, the Comasterids differ from the other families of feather-stars in having the mouth off-set to one side with the anus taking its place almost in the centre. Two-thirds of the Comasterid species are multibrachiate, though the rest have ten arms. This contrasts with families such as the Antedonidae, in which multibrachiate species are very rare.

A species of *Echinometra*, probably the most common sea-urchin genus of tropical reefs. *Echinometra* species, like the related *Heterocentrotus* species, have the test oval rather than circular. Photo by Allan Power.

Strongylocentrotus franciscanus, a common sea-urchin of Californian kelp beds. Photo by T.E. Thompson.

All the present-day crinoids, both stalked and free, are usually considered as belonging to a single order, the Articulata. In comparison, two orders are recognized for the living Ophiuroids, five for the Asteroids, five for the Holothurians and as many as fifteen in the latest assessment for the Echinoids.

The order Articulata is divided into four sub-orders, of which one—the Comatulida—includes all the feather-stars. The fifteen families are arranged in two groups but superficially there are no very striking differences between them. Among the attached crinoids, those like *Metacrinus* with stalks bearing cirri form one sub-order, another includes *Rhizocrinus* and other genera with root-like attachments together with some genera which have expanded bases to the stalks, while the last sub-order includes some other attached forms lacking cirri as well as the extraordinary genus *Holopus* which deserves special mention.

The single known species, *Holopus rangi*, was first described as long ago as 1837 but still only about a dozen specimens of it have been recorded. All of them came from the West Indian area and from depths of about 100 fathoms, with the possible exception of one said to have been caught on a fishing line in only five fathoms. Superficially *Holopus* resembles a model of a mailed fist, having a massive wrist-like basal piece, making up about a third of the total height and bearing five axillary plates around its upper edge, each carrying a pair of short, stout, strongly incurved arms, fitting together to form a tight 'fist'. In the largest known specimen, which is only about four cm. high, two of the axillaries are preceded by an additional segment; otherwise the single basal piece is presumably formed by fusion of all the pre-axillary plates including the radials, basals and centrodorsal, perhaps some stalk plates as well. The base is always expanded at the bottom and closely moulded to grip the underlying rock. It is hollow and the disc with the digestive tract and other organs is recessed into it. The mouth opens in the centre of the disc and is surrounded by five large triangular plates, resembling and possibly homologous with the oral plates of a larval feather-star. In preserved specimens the contraction and in-coiling of the arms results in complete concealment and protection of the disc. An unusual feature is the asymmetrical shape caused by the larger size of the arms and axillaries of one side than those of the other. In the largest specimens each of the longer arms has eight to ten exposed segments, as opposed to six or seven in the shorter arms. These exposed arm segments taper markedly so that all the arms fit together tightly in the centre. The distal part of each arm is abruptly constricted laterally and coils in and down out of sight and back under itself within the cavity formed by the exposed parts. The pinnules are short, broad and flattened, as well as being curled directly under the arm, instead of standing out from it as in other crinoids. This results in the formation of an almost continuous tube along the underside of each arm, since the consecutive pinnules from alternate sides fit closely together.

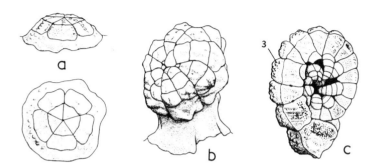

Fig. 25. *Holopus rangi.* a) Presumed juvenile form in side and upper view, b) young specimen in side view, showing the 'lop-sided' shape owing to the different lengths of the arms and c) side view of a single arm with its axillary, from a larger specimen, showing the coiled position and the incurled pinnules; the pinnules on brachials 3 and 5 have been broken at the first joint to reveal the distal part of the arm. [Magnifications a) ×20, b) ×10 and c) ×6.] (After Carpenter)

When feeding *Holopus* presumably extends its arms like other crinoids and feeds by passing a current of water through the pinnule tubes impelled by the usual ciliary action.

A single specimen believed to be a juvenile *Holopus* has also been discovered. This is only one millimetre high but three millimetres wide at the base, resembling a tortoise-shell in shape, with the central part apparently formed of two concentric rings, each of five plates, the inner ones wedge-shaped and the whole surrounded by an individual basal mass. The ten central plates probably represent the rudiments of five arms and as growth proceeds, the other five arms could be developed in between.

Possibly *Holopus* may prove to be not uncommon in the waters around Barbados and Martinique (the source of the known specimens). Its

Above: *Bohadschia argus*, a tropical Pacific aspidochirotid with very distinctive spotted colouration. Photo by Keith Gillett.

Left: *Stichopus variegatus*, a stout-bodied tropical Indo-West Pacific aspidochirotid; the inconspicuous tentacles are not visible here. Photo by Keith Gillett.

Parastichopus parvimensis, an East Pacific aspidochirotid having the tube feet of the upper side pointed and lacking terminal sucking discs. Photo by Dan Gotschall.

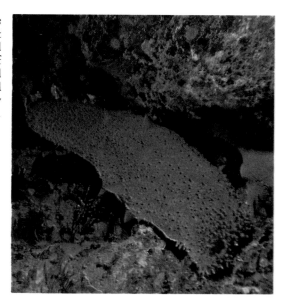

Opheodesoma species, a thin-skinned apodid holothurian with large pinnate tentacles (right). The dark lines correspond with the five longitudinal muscle bands. Photo by Aaron Norman.

squat shape and strong attachment to the underlying rock obviously make it a difficult animal to catch in a trawl. We can only hope that better methods of collecting may be devised so that a good range of specimens showing the whole life history may be obtained.

Holopus is one of the smallest present-day crinoids, growing to a height of only about four cm. Most of the large sea-lilies with cirri, like *Metacrinus*, reach a stalk length of about 60 cm., with the calyx and arms adding another 15 cm. or so. This size is puny compared with that of certain extinct species which are estimated to have had stalk lengths exceeding 20 meters. *Rhizocrinus* and most other recent genera lacking cirri are usually very slender and in *Rhizocrinus lofotensis* the stalk length does not exceed about seven cm. with the calyx and arms less than 12 mm. Among the feather-stars, the Comasterids and other tropical forms are some of the most massive, with arm lengths commonly about 25 cm. or even more, so that the diameter may approach 60 cm. In a multibrachiate species with over a hundred arms the resultant bulk may be considerable. Few of the Antedonidae are conspicuous for their size, larger specimens of *Antedon bifida* having arms about 12 cm. long. Exceptions are the arctic species *Heliometra glacialis* and its antarctic relatives such as *Florometra* and *Promachocrinus*. *Heliometra* grows to a great size in the Okhotsk and Japan Seas, the largest specimen recorded having an arm length of 350 mm. or a span ·of over 60 cm., though with only ten arms the absolute bulk is not so great as in the multibrachiate Comasterids.

As for the colour, since crinoids are unappetizing creatures with little need for concealment, this is often bright with reds and purples predominating. Another name formerly given to *Antedon bifida* was *rosacea*, though its colour range is from yellow and orange to purple. Some tropical species are very lurid with bold patterns of purple and yellow, while others are white or black or have various combinations of colours, often forming beautiful radiating patterns. A few colder water species such as *Heliometra glacialis* and *Leptometra celtica* differ in being green, though olive and even blue are found in some warm water forms. Exceptions to these bold colours occur in most deep-sea crinoids living beyond the reach of daylight, which, tend to be more drab and uniform in colour.

Unfortunately crinoids, though so attractive in life, are among the most difficult Echinoderms to preserve. Their colours are quickly lost, and the arms, cirri and pinnules break into fragments very easily. Even in aquaria they require optimum conditions of aeration, temperature and salinity or they will soon disintegrate and die.

FEEDING

Like most other major groups of animals, Echinoderms feed in a variety of ways and on many different kinds of food. The majority eat only small particles of edible matter, which are either suspended in the water or lying as detritus on the bottom, while many species that burrow in the soft parts of the sea-bed actually swallow quantities of mud or sand and digest the edible matter from it. However, a number of forms among the brittle-stars, sea-urchins and particularly the starfishes, have become omnivorous or even carnivorous, feeding by scavenging or grazing on the plant and animal life around them, or by attacking prey of quite large size compared with themselves, as with the notorious kinds of starfish that menace mussel and oyster beds.

Feather-Stars

The method of feeding in crinoids is believed to be more primitive than that of any other Echinoderm. Their food is restricted to small bits of detritus and to planktonic micro-organisms, both animal and plant, such as protozoans, various larvae, small crustaceans, diatoms and algae.

In order to catch this varied material a feather-star such as *Antedon* fixes itself securely with its cirri and stretches out its arms sideways with the pinnules extended almost at right angles, making an extensive kind of net, since the proximal pinnules of adjacent arms overlap. The ambulacral grooves running from the mouth along the upper side of each arm give off a branch to each pinnule and these grooves are bordered by tentacles or podia, usually arising in groups of three. When stimulated by contact with edible particles in the water, the extended podia flick inwards and drive any nearby particle into the groove to be trapped in quantities of mucus secreted by special glands. The mucus is passed in a stream towards the mouth by current set up by the beating of countless minute, whip-like cilia along the grooves. The oral pinnules, that is those nearest the mouth, usually have no ambulacral groove of their own and are modified for some other function. It is known that in certain species, where they are particularly long and flexible near the tips, the oral pinnules assist in catching larger and more active prey such as small crustaceans.

The effectiveness of the crinoid method of feeding depends on the total length of the food groove relative to the mass of the entire crinoid. When the lengths of the grooves along the pinnules are added to those

103

Psolus chitonoides, a dendrochirotid from the Pacific coast of North America, resembling an armour-plated slug; the vulnerable crown of bushy tentacles can be completely retracted. Photo by T.E. Thompson.

Below: *Parastichopus californicus,* an especially gherkin-like holothurian from the northeast Pacific. Photo by T.E. Thompson.

Pseudocolochirus axiologus, a brightly colored tropical Pacific cucumariid from northern Australia, showing the very large branching tentacles extended and the tube feet restricted to the red-coloured ambulacra. Photo by Roger Steene.

along the arms, an amazingly high total may be reached. For instance, a specimen of the large Japanese stalked crinoid *Metacrinus rotundus*, with 56 arms each about 20 cm. long, was estimated to have a total groove length of about 75 meters, while a multi-armed tropical feather-star of the species *Comantheria grandicalyx*, with 68 arms each about 12 cm. long, has a groove length probably of over 100 meters. Even among the ten-armed species, *Antedon* has a groove length of about 17 meters when the arm length is only 11 cm., while the large arctic *Heliometra glacialis* has the total length about 55 meters when the arms are 20 cm. long.

The Echinoderms other than Crinoids have the ambulacra partly if not entirely on the under side, and their methods of feeding are necessarily different, though ciliary action and the secretion of mucus play a major part in some species.

Brittle-stars and basket-stars

Most brittle-stars, like the crinoids, feed on detritus and on microscopic plant or animal matter suspended or swimming in the water near the bottom, catching the food particles in quantities of sticky mucus secreted by numerous glands along the arms. Here again the mucus is carried by ciliary current in a stream towards the mouth, and the podia give some degree of assistance in 'handling' the food. Many of the Amphiurids and other species which burrow into sand or mud live with the disc and mouth below the surface, but the outer parts of their arms may project and sweep about, catching up any available detritus.

However, some ophiuroids are at least partly carnivorous and catch small worms and crustaceans with the flexible arm tips. The trapped prey is then passed to the mouth, either by the series of podia or by bending the entire arm inwards. The basket-stars like *Gorgonocephalus*, with their much-branched, very mobile arms, present a formidable food-catching mechanism. When at rest, the slender, tendril-like, small branches of the arms are coiled up into bunches, but if the basket-star is hungry, or stimulated by contact with the small swimming animals, notably crustaceans, on which it feeds, the arms stretch out sideways and upwards, forming a bowl-shaped openwork basket. Since these ophiuroids grow to a diameter of over 60 cm., the ramifications of the arms may cover a very large area. As each small branch is touched by a shrimp or other suitable prey, it quickly coils around and seizes it, helped by other branches nearby, if necessary. When several organisms have been caught in this way the entire arm may be bent inwards toward the mouth to pass on the food.

Sea-cucumbers

Similar actions are involved in the feeding of many sea-cucumbers, particularly the Dendrochirota such as *Cucumaria*. In holothurians the ring of tentacles around the mouth has taken over from the tube feet the function of obtaining food. *Cucumaria* catches particles of detritus with its large branching tentacles, entraps them in mucus and passes them to the mouth by successively incurling the tentacles. In *Holothuria* the tentacles are relatively smaller and simply scoop the surrounding material, detritus, mud or sand, into the mouth, while burrowing forms like *Leptosynapta* engulf and swallow the substrate as they plough along through it. From study of various species of *Holothuria* on a certain coral reef, it was estimated that the population of about 2,000 sea-cucumbers inhabiting each acre of the reef, between them passed over 60 tons of sand and other bottom material through their digestive tracts each year.

Starfishes

Many starfishes too live on detritus or living micro-organisms. All of them have some development of cilia on certain areas of the skin and these beat in concert to set up currents running in particular directions. Those on the dorsal surface at least usually run towards the margin, though there may be eddy currents or others encircling the larger spines. In most species the function of these currents is mainly respiratory and sanitary in that they keep the water moving over the surface and clean off unwanted debris falling on the body. However, some starfishes have elaborated the system to enable edible particles to be passed to the mouth for swallowing instead of being rejected. Feeding, at least partly by this method, is well developed in genera such as *Luidia* and *Astropecten*, while in *Ctenodiscus* and *Porania* for instance, it is of primary importance. *Porania* has conspicuous grooves in the ventral skin leading from the margin towards the ambulacral furrows (Plate VI, fig. f), while the other genera have the underlying plates modified to form channels fringed with spinelets leading between the marginal plates and between the ventral plates. In these grooves or channels the current sets in general downwards at the margin and then in towards the mouth. The particles of matter are caught in strings of mucus, secreted by associated glands and moved along by ciliary action. In *Ctenodiscus*, the stomach and hence the whole body is usually found distended with swallowed mud, but the other genera do not appear to gorge themselves to this extent.

The efficiency of this method of feeding has been demonstrated by the indefinite survival without loss of weight of starfishes like *Porania* in

A large Indo-Pacific feather-star, probably a Himerometra species, showing enlarged and modified proximal pinnules covering the vulnerable soft disc and the zig-zag ambulacral grooves along the upper sides of the arms. Photo by Dr. Herbert R. Axelrod.

Opposite:
Arm tips of a feather-star with particularly short discoidal arm segments and stout, blunt-tipped pinnules. Photo by Dr. Gerald R. Allen.

aquaria with a supply of constantly renewed sea-water containing microscopic organic matter but with no source of larger food. In the same situation, the carnivorous *Asterias* loses weight rapidly and starves to death in about eight weeks.

Although *Luidia* and *Astropecten* are among the starfishes which have ciliary currents capable of carrying food to the mouth in this way, their diet is much more nearly omnivorous, ranging from algae, worms, sponges, other echinoderms and crustaceans to molluscs which are not too big to be swallowed whole but which may be so bulky that they distort the centre of the disc of the starfish (Plate XIII, fig. a). Both these genera have tube feet which are pointed at the tip, so that they are incapable of dealing with larger bivalved molluscs in the manner of those starfishes which have strong sucking discs on the tube feet to grasp and pull on the shells of their prey.

An interesting carnivorous type is the very flattened goose-foot starfish *Anseropoda*. Examinations of its stomach contents have revealed only the presence of such animals as relatively large and active crustaceans including shrimps, water fleas and small swimming crabs. Unfortunately no-one has yet observed just how *Anseropoda* manages to capture such quick-moving prey.

Other starfishes with unlikely sources of food include the large tropical, multi-rayed *Acanthaster* (Plate VI, fig. g), which feeds on coral polyps, leaving in its wake a trail of dead coral, and the West Indian *Oreaster* (Plate II, figs. a–d), which has only been seen to eat sponges.

A very voracious species is *Pycnopodia helianthoides*, found in shallow water from California to Alaska. It has up to 24 arms and reaches a diameter of nearly a meter. Its food is largely hermit-crabs and sea-urchins, which are grasped by the tube feet and swallowed whole, even the urchins with their formidable sharp spines. After a day or two, the empty test and the detached spines are thrown out, all the rest having been digested. In a large *Pycnopodia* the total number of tube feet has been estimated at about 15,000, so there are plenty to mobilize in tackling its prey.

By far the most interesting and widely studied method of feeding in starfishes is that used by the common *Asterias* for the capture and assimilation of bivalved molluscs, such as oysters and mussels, which are often of such relatively large size that they cannot be swallowed. Instead they are digested externally by the very thin-walled stomach of the starfish. This is everted through the mouth and inserted between the two shells of the mollusc, enwrapping and digesting the soft body *in situ*. Most of the starfishes which feed in this way have four rows of

Feeding

tube feet along the ambulacral groove of each arm, as in *Asterias*.
However, other genera such as *Solaster*, also menace the oyster beds
though their tube feet are only in two rows, but in this case the number
of feet is increased by those of the many additional arms. This emphasis
on the feet is made because they usually play a large part in opening the
bivalve against the opposition of its strong adductor muscle which is
designed to keep the shells tightly shut. Since closure of the shells is
usually the only defence of these molluscs against the onset of unfavourable conditions, such as the retreat of the water at low tide or
attack by a predator such as the starfish, this muscle is necessarily a very
powerful one.

There have been a number of theories as to how the starfish manages
to overcome the pull of the adductor muscle. One possibility is that the
extruded stomach produces a poison which either relaxes or weakens
the muscle of the prey. To test this, experiments were performed in
Japan with a species of *Asterias*. The stomach tissue of the starfish was
ground up and added to the water in which the hearts of bivalves were
exposed. This proved to have a toxic effect on the hearts whereas the
stomach extract of herbivorous species of starfishes did not. However,
similar stomach extracts from a species of *Astropecten* also had a toxic
effect. *Astropecten* is carnivorous too but swallows its prey whole. It is
possible then that the toxic effect is correlated with the presence of an
enzyme in the stomach for digesting animal food and does not imply
that a special poison is present to induce the opening of the mollusc.
The experiments are therefore inconclusive and they have yet to be
supported by the results of biochemical studies.

The present evidence seems to indicate rather that two distinct
methods of feeding on bivalves can be employed according to the
circumstances and that neither of these involves any chemical secretion
other than that of the digestive enzymes.[1]

If the bivalve is not too large, as with mussels having a shell length
equal to not more than a quarter of the diameter of the starfish and if
both of its shells are accessible, then it is opened by force alone. The starfish straddles the bivalve, manipulates it with the tube feet to a convenient position, usually with the hinge on the far side from the starfish's
mouth, the tube feet of the inner parts of the arms fix their sucking discs
on to both shells while those of the rest of the arms grip the surrounding
sea-floor, the centre of the starfish arches up so that the feet holding
the shell are stretched, and a sustained pull begins by contraction of the

[1] Feder, *Ecology*, vol. 36, pp. 764–767, 1955; Christensen, *Limnology and Oceanography*, vol. 2, pp. 180–197, 1957; Burnett, *Ecology*, vol. 41, pp. 583–584, 1960.

A multi-armed feather-star, the anchoring cirri concealed by the out-stretched arms in the foreground. Photo by H. Cogger.

Opposite:
A single arm regenerating to form a comet-like individual of a *Linckia* species. The number of new arms is more often five than four. Photo by Dr. Herbert R. Axelrod.

Plate XII. A starfish eating a small fish in an aquarium; the semi-transparent stomach of the starfish can be seen partly enveloping the fish. (After Bailey, *Natural History*, New York, volume 66)

longitudinal muscles of each foot. In observations of starfishes about 38 cm. in diameter, with bivalves about 5 cm. long, it was often only about twenty minutes, sometimes even less, before a significant gaping of the shells was observed. Once this movement had begun, within a very few minutes (averaging about eight) the shells were steadily pulled apart to a gape of from one to twenty millimetres and the stomach was then inserted through the gap created. The proof that force alone was used lies in experiments where the shells of bivalves, with their adductor muscles previously severed and so ineffective, were held closed by rubber bands but yet were successfully opened by starfishes. Similar results were obtained using dummy bivalves baited with mussel flesh inside and held shut by a system of weights whereby the actual strength of the pull exerted by the starfish could be measured. With starfishes about 30 cm. in diameter this pull was found to be equivalent to a total of about eight pounds. Confirmation that force is used is provided by the discovery of bivalves being eaten in which the adductor muscles have actually been torn.

Once the starfish's stomach has been inserted between the shells, it proceeds to digest the mollusc for between seven and fifteen hours according to size. When the meal is finished the starfish simply moves away leaving the empty shell behind. As an example of persistence, in one experiment with dummy bivalves needing a pull of about eleven pounds to open them, starfishes about 50 cm. in diameter were finally successful after two nights and a day of sustained effort. (These experiments were usually begun at night since the starfishes used were normally nocturnal feeders.)

On the other hand, if the starfish found the bivalve to be either too large for force alone to be effective, or else to be lying in an inaccessible position (such as in a cavity, or on the far side of a rigid net, or fixed to the bottom so that one or both of the shells were out of reach of the tube feet), then a different method of attack was adopted. Many bivalves, such as mussels, have a permanent opening between the shells near the hinge for the passage of the threads by which they attach themselves. In Californian mussels, this opening was found to be 0·3–3·2 mm. across. By experiments with bivalves in which the shells were bound round with steel wire and impossible to open, it has been shown that starfishes are quite capable of insinuating their stomachs through apertures as small as or even smaller than this, since an oyster with imperfect shells having a gap only 0·2 mm. wide was partly digested. The size of the hole of course limits the amount of stomach that can be inserted through it; consequently, feeding by this method takes much longer than when the shells

115

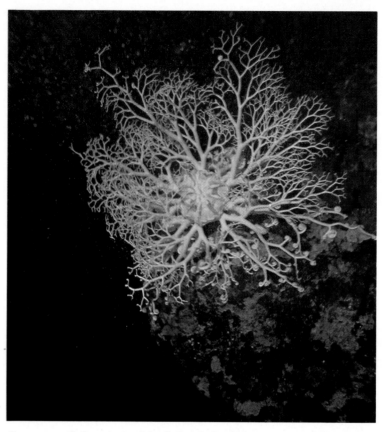

Gorgonocephalus caryi, a North Pacific basket-star; some of the smaller branches of one arm are bunched up in feeding. Photo by Dan Gotschall.

The comparatively large pedicellariae of a *Toxopneustes* species, capable of imparting intense pain to the unwary toucher. Photo by Keith Gillett.

are opened by force and the whole stomach can be employed. The time for digestion may be as long as 22 hours and often the prey is abandoned only partly digested.

The total quantity of food eaten by these carnivorous starfishes may be considerable. For instance, in natural conditions it has been calculated that in two days a young *Asterias* can eat the equivalent of its own volume in bivalves.

These voracious starfishes do not necessarily limit themselves to feeding on mussels and oysters but will tackle any suitable animal not too active to escape them. Some bivalves, such as scallops, can usually get away by swimming since they are very sensitive to contact with the exploratory terminal tube feet of a starfish and are warned in time. In the artificial conditions and confined space of an aquarium even fishes if moribund or merely lethargic may be caught and eaten by starfishes (Plate XII).

In grasping objects like fishes or crustaceans with surfaces roughened by scales or fine processes, *Asterias* may use its pedicellariae as well as the tube feet to get a good hold.

Other starfishes which habitually digest their food externally include cushion-stars such as the large North Pacific *Patiria miniata* and the small European *Asterina gibbosa*. *Patiria* has a particularly big stomach that is commonly found to be everted. It cannot deal with large shelled prey but eats almost anything else, from minute encrusting algae to sedentary animals, including other members of its own species. In an aquarium one *Patiria* about ten cm. in diameter has been seen to digest a second one nearly five cm. across down to its constituent skeletal plates in a period of only about 35 hours. Oddly enough it was found by experiment that the digestive juices or enzymes capable of dissolving flesh so efficiently are not secreted by the stomach itself but by ten paired sacs, two in each radius, which branch off the upper part of the stomach and are retained inside the body. These are called the digestive glands or pyloric caecae, and the enzymes they produce are carried by ciliary currents on to the lining of the stomach, even when this is everted.

Sea-urchins

The regular sea-urchins are mostly omnivorous browsers and scavengers, feeding on almost anything they come across (even including each other if starved in an aquarium) though some have a preference for either plant or animal food. To deal with such a variety of material they have developed a very powerful chewing mechanism. This consists of five

Plate XIII. a) A tropical *Astropecten* with the disc and the base of one arm distended by a large cone shell which it has swallowed; b) the lower half of the test of a sea-urchin showing the chewing apparatus or Aristotle's lantern

Pedicellariae and spines around the apex of the sea-urchin *Lytechinus williamsi*, from the Atlantic side of Panama. Photo by T.E. Thompson.

The starfish *Pisaster ochraceus* and sea-urchin *Strongylocentrotus*, common inshore inhabitants of Pacific coastal waters of the United States. Photo by T.E. Thompson.

Side view of *Pisaster ochraceus*. The expanded respiratory papulae show as purple in colour, contrasting with the red network of the skeleton and the white-tipped short spines. Photo by T.E. Thompson.

large, vertically aligned teeth supported by an internal framework of skeletal bars and operated by strong muscles. In describing this structure Aristotle compared it with a lantern with the panes left out all round; consequently it is generally called Aristotle's lantern (Plate XIII, fig. b). The tips of the teeth are just visible through the mouth. They wear away with constant usage and are replaced from above by the downward shifting of the entire tooth, to which new growth is added at the upper end. With this mechanism the sea-urchin can scrape off and crunch up encrusting and other growths from the bottom, including such apparently inedible matter as barnacles, hydroids, tube worms, sponges and various sea-weeds, as well as smaller algae.

The regular sea-urchins in a similar way to certain starfishes also collect as food any particles of edible matter falling on their upper surfaces. These particles are passed to the mouth by the tube feet, by the spines and particularly by certain of the small, forceps-like pedicellariae scattered over the body. The pedicellariae with their long flexible stalks may also catch live prey such as small crustaceans, while the globiferous ones, with their poison glands, can paralyse the catch by injecting their secretion.

In contrast, the irregular sea-urchins live buried in the sand or mud, and have lost (or in the case of cake-urchins modified) the teeth. Their food consists of small particles of organic matter in the surrounding sand or mud, usually passed to the mouth by the combined efforts of specialized tube feet, ciliary currents and mucus streams along the ambulacra. The gut becomes filled with the skeletons of minute organisms and other particles, so that its course inside the test is clearly visible in an X-ray photograph.

REGENERATION

All living things have some capacity for repair and replacement or regeneration of damaged or lost parts, though the extent of this varies enormously in different groups of animals. At the least it is confined to healing of relatively small wounds, as in man, but in some animals entire limbs can be replaced, while in others, usually of rather simple organization, such as flat-worms and Coelenterates, almost the entire body may be reconstituted from a small piece. Even within the phylum Echinodermata there is a wide range in the possible extent of regeneration and in the rate at which it takes place, these factors being usually correlated with the relative fragility of the species. For instance, particularly robust species which rarely suffer serious injury, such as the tropical starfishes of the family Oreasteridae, can do little more than heal over the open wound left when an arm is severed. However, most Echinoderms are more liable to suffer damage or loss, and the power of regeneration has been fostered in them by natural selection. The majority of starfishes are capable of replacing one or more lost arms, while some can also regenerate parts of the disc, sometimes as much as half of it; exceptionally even the entire disc as well as the other arms can be regenerated from a single arm.

The maximum capability in this respect is reached by some tropical starfishes of the family Ophidiasteridae. Even part of an arm of certain species of *Linckia* can survive when broken off from the rest, and grow a complete new disc and arms at the severed end. This results at first in what is called a 'comet form', since the original arm resembles a long tail with the new little star at its base. When a mouth and digestive organs have been developed, the new starfish can start feeding and growth becomes rapid. The new arms gradually enlarge to about the same size as the old one. Most extraordinary of all is the fact that specimens of a few species like *Linckia columbiae*, from the west coast of Mexico and California, will deliberately break off one of their arms for no apparent reason. This phenomenon is called autotomy. *Linckia* has a particularly tough body wall with a well-developed skeleton, but when one arm simply walks away from the others while they hold fast, pulling against it, the tissues become stretched, usually at a point a short distance from the disc, until the body wall finally breaks under the strain.

Since autotomy and regeneration result in an increase in the starfish population, the process can be classed as asexual reproduction. In *Linckia columbiae* it is so common that symmetrical specimens with all the arms identical in size are very hard to find.

123

Pisaster brevispinus, a large Californian relative of *Asterias,* which can be safely handled. Photo by T.E. Thompson.

An agitated sea-cucumber, *Holothuria leucospilota*, which has ejected its gut and thread-like sticky Cuvierian tubules as a defence reaction. Photo by T.E. Thompson.

Patiria miniata, a North Pacific starfish, showing the (temporary) leading arm raised and testing the environment. Photo by Dr. Herbert R. Axelrod.

a   b

Plate XIV. Regeneration: a) comet form of *Linckia*, with five arms regenerating from one and b) *Nepanthia* with four arms regenerating from three after dividing across the disc

Some starfishes other than *Linckia* can survive and grow anew from a single arm, but only if a part of the disc remains attached to it. *Asterias rubens* can do this if necessary, although it probably does not undergo autotomy spontaneously, only if subjected to adverse conditions.

There are also starfishes like *Nepanthia briareus* (Plate XIV, fig. b) and the Mediterranean *Coscinasterias tenuispina*, as well as brittle-stars like *Ophiactis savignyi* (fig. 26b) which regularly reproduce asexually; they split in two across the disc and each half then regenerates the arms and part of the disc that it lacks. Species which undergo spontaneous fission like this are called fissiparous. They nearly always have more than five arms, as well as more than one madreporite, and in some starfishes also more than one anus, so that, after dividing, the two parts each have at least one madreporite and possibly an anus as well. However, it does not necessarily follow that the cause of division is physical instability

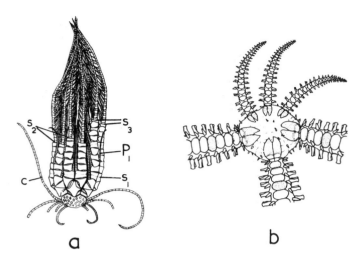

Fig. 26. a) Feather-star *Heliometra glacialis* with all the arms in process of regeneration from syzygies, the second syzygy of the left centre arm being abnormally placed, consisting of brachials 10 + 11 instead of 9 + 10; (P_1) first pinnule, (*c*) cirrus, (s_1, s_2, s_3) first three syzygies, b) brittle-star *Ophiactis savignyi* regenerating half the disc and three arms

produced by the multiplicity of arms and madreporites together, since the multi-armed starfish *Acanthaster* may have nearly as many madreporites as arms but is not fissiparous.

In some of the brittle-star and starfish species which are fissiparous both five- and six-armed individuals, apparently of the same species, are found, the five-armed ones rarely showing signs of fission whereas all those with six arms are more or less obviously in process of regeneration. Since the only large specimens of these species are some of those with five arms, several authorities have assumed that the six-armed young give rise to the five-armed adult by only regenerating two arms from a half with three, following one division. However, there is as yet no proof that the number of arms may change from five to six and back again to five during the life history of an individual. The large five-armed specimens could be the survivors of those few which have always been five-armed while those which have been six-armed since metamorphosis are unstable and simply continue to divide and regenerate endlessly with the same number of arms so that they never reach a large size. It is possible that some five-armed ones when young may be induced to divide by abnormal conditions, and this may account for the

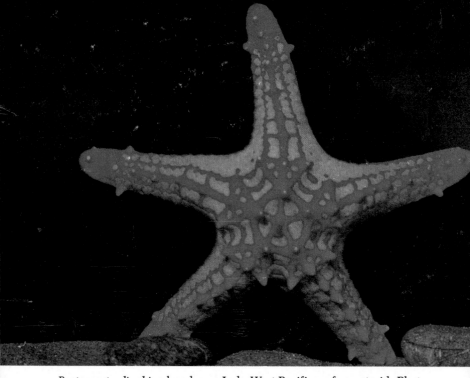

Protoreaster lincki, a handsome Indo-West Pacific reef oreasterid. Photo by Dr. S. Frank.

Two *Asterias* feeding on mussels. Photo by Aaron Norman.

occasional specimens observed with two large arms and four small ones regenerating.

Until breeding experiments are carried out on some of these species the problem will remain unanswered.

A few autotomous species are also known among sea-cucumbers such as *Leptosynapta inhaerens* and *Cucumaria planci*, both found in British waters. These constrict themselves transversely and twist or pull apart into two or more pieces, each usually regenerating as an entire cucumber. Here again this habit appears to be more common among, or even restricted to, immature specimens, particularly when subjected to adverse conditions.

Many other species of holothurian commonly regenerate the larger part of their internal organs, following the rupture and evisceration provoked by attacks on them, or by the onset of unfavourable conditions.

Crinoids are also very liable to eviscerate themselves, the whole of the soft parts within the calyx cup being cast off and readily grown anew from tissue in the bottom of the cup. Similarly, some brittle-stars are often found with the whole disc in process of regeneration. This is particularly common among the burrowing Amphiurids, following the distention of the disc by genital products during the breeding season. In some cases rupture or shedding of the disc accompanies escape of the eggs or embryos.

Parts of the arms, or even entire arms, may also be shed by crinoids and brittle-stars under stress or following damage to them. The syzygies or special breaking joints of crinoids which aid this practice have already been mentioned.

Regular sea-urchins with their compact body form and usually stout skeleton are rarely found with the test itself damaged, but if necessary they can repair holes in it, though it is doubtful whether they could survive the loss or breakage of more than about a fifth of the body. Their spines, pedicellariae and tube feet, however, all regenerate readily, being more liable to loss or damage. Under adverse conditions, such as stagnation of the water, a sea-urchin may shed its spines only to grow them anew if conditions return to normal while it is still alive.

Some of the flatter cake-urchins such as *Mellita* (Plate IX, fig. a) are often found with irregular margins, particularly around the posterior edge. Probably many cases of this sort of damage can be explained by the assumption that some predator has taken a bite at them, since they are fed upon by a number of other animals including certain fishes as well as starfishes. The posterior end is more vulnerable than the anterior since it may remain exposed when the front end has burrowed into the sand.

ADAPTATIONS FOR DEFENCE

Because of their prominent armour of plates and often spines as well, most Echinoderms would appear to be unpalatable, to say the least. Nevertheless, so great is the struggle for survival that certain marine animals do feed on some of them. Notable among such predators are those fishes that seek their food on the sea bottom; for instance, soles are often found with brittle-stars in their stomachs, while cod and haddock will even tackle sea-urchins. In addition, other Echinoderms, as well as crabs, boring molluscs, sea-birds and marine mammals, may account for many of the casualties.

In the crinoids the skeleton is so massive that almost the only part of the body that is edible is the small central disc. This is fairly well protected by the calyx and arm bases around it, but some species of feather-stars have spike-like oral pinnules that project upwards around the disc and probably have a protective function.

Most sea-urchins have a bristly coat of spike-like spines all over their tests. Some of them, like the European *Paracentrotus lividus*, live in aggregations, together presenting a formidable array of armament. The chief enemy of *Paracentrotus* in the Mediterranean is probably man, who can grapple it with tools and break it open to extract the tasty roes. Another sea-urchin, *Strongylocentrotus*, from colder waters, forms an important part of the food of sea-otters along the Pacific coasts of North America. This is particularly interesting as it is one of the few examples of the use of tools by animals other than man. The otters collect several sea-urchins off the bottom, together with a piece of rock. Coming to the surface, they float on their backs and using their fore paws, smash the tests open against the rock, with their own chests acting as a table. Sometimes they do without a rock and simply hold one urchin between the paws and strike it against another on the chest. *Strongylocentrotus* is also fed upon by the arctic fox, eider duck and crows, which pull them off the rocks at low tide. The crows have been seen to drop the urchins from a height on to the rocks so that the tests break open and they can pick out the soft parts. Other predators include fishes with crushing teeth like the cod, as well as the large Pacific starfish *Pycnopodia*, which swallows the urchins whole regardless of their spines.

There are some tropical genera, however, which have such a formidable array of spines that only well-armoured kinds of fishes will attack. These include *Diadema* and *Echinothrix*, both with very slender, brittle spines, the upper ones usually longer than the test is wide (Plate XV). They have a speedy response to changes in light intensity, the spines being quickly

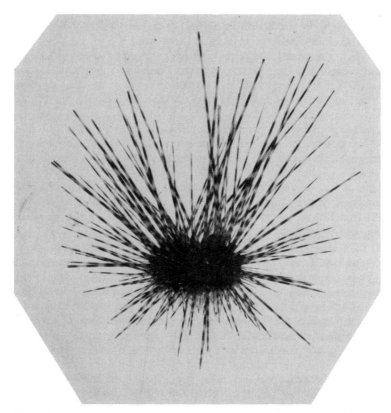

Plate XV. A young specimen of the tropical sea-urchin *Diadema*, with the long defensive spines banded light and dark

pointed in the direction of any threatening obstruction to the light. If something like a human foot impales itself upon them, they usually break off in the wound and are almost impossible to pull out. In addition, they are barbed along their whole length and in *Echinothrix* the barbs are inclined backwards so that removal is even more difficult. As if this were not enough, the skin around the spines is glandular and secretes a strong irritant substance, visible as a reddish fluid when the spine is broken. This aggravates the pain of the physical injury, which would be bad enough in itself. Since the spines are dark in colour they are visible in the flesh. Those of the West Indian *Diadema antillarum* dissolve and disappear within a few days, but the spines of the related Indo-Pacific species are said to persist for several weeks. A recommended treatment is to hasten the process of dissolution by pressure, to try and break up the spines into smaller fragments in the wound!

There is another Indo-Pacific echinoid not closely related to *Diadema*, but capable of inflicting even more pain, although its spines are quite small in comparison with the diameter of the test. This is called *Asthenosoma varium*, and it belongs to the only genus of the family Echinothuriidae to be found in shallow water. The whole family is characterized by the flexible articulation of the test plates so that Echinothuriids brought out of the sea are liable to collapse into flat pancakes, although in life they are inflated and almost rigid. The smaller secondary spines of the upper surface of *Asthenosoma* are those responsible for its evil reputation among Japanese pearl divers. Each has a blue coloured contractile poison sac around its tip, so that the poison is injected through the puncture made by the tip of the spine when touched by a foreign body.

In neither *Diadema* nor *Asthenosoma* are pedicellariae of the globiferous kind found, but in the genus *Toxopneustes*, also from tropical waters, these organs are numerous and also relatively very large, the distance between the fangs of the three valves when fully opened being up to 4 mm. The bases of the valves are usually coloured a bright purple, and this, together with the petal-like form of the large poison glands associated with each valve, gives the whole sea-urchin the misleading appearance of a posy of flowers. However, should any part of the skin thin enough to be punctured touch it, then the fangs of the pedicellariae would quickly bring disillusion about their innocence. A Japanese biologist, 'stung' on the side of a finger by only seven or eight pedicellariae, when taking a *Toxopneustes* from a diver, experienced intense pain and irritation, giddiness, difficulty in breathing and partial facial paralysis, the last persisting for several hours. It can be imagined that serious consequences might result from a diver having a brush with one of these urchins while submerged, and the pearl divers are very wary of them. Although no authentic case of death from such contact is known, it may possibly account for a few of the unexplained fatal casualties.

Even the tiny globiferous pedicellariae of certain other genera related to *Toxopneustes*, each only about one millimetre across the jaws, can combine to produce a very painful rash on uncalloused areas of skin such as on the backs of the hands and the arms, taking as much as a month to disappear. Most temperate species of sea-urchins have relatively few pedicellariae of this toxic kind, so there is little risk of this happening.

Plate XVI. The tropical sea-urchin *Toxopneustes*, showing the large triangular globiferous pedicellariae

Individual pedicellariae are very mobile on their long stalks. Since they are linked by the peripheral network of nerves, a number of neighbouring ones can concentrate on any local contact. They are extraordinarily tenacious and are often broken off at the stalk while retaining their grip on the aggressor. If a predator such as a large starfish perseveres, then by repeated attacks it may deplete the armament of globiferous pedicellariae to such an extent that the sea-urchin is overcome, even though it had successfully repulsed the initial attack.

Among the starfishes a number of species of the order Forcipulata, including *Asterias* and *Marthasterias*, have large extensible sheaths of very numerous, though small, two-valved pedicellariae around the spines. *Pycnopodia* from the west coast of North America, has these

133

wreaths so well developed that they can 'sting' the back of ones hand just like the globiferous pedicellariae of an echinoid. Judging from this, the glandular tissue associated with the pedicellariae of *Pycnopodia* must produce a similar irritant secretion. Though less well adapted to inject this secretion, the starfish pedicellariae make up for that by their multiplicity. In *Odinella nutrix* from the Southern Ocean, belonging to the family Brisingidae, the larger spines are each enveloped in a complete sac of skin studded with hordes of very tiny crossed pedicellariae, each little more than a tenth of a millimetre long. Unfortunately nothing is yet known about the way these are used in life.

Many other starfishes and echinoids with inadequate armaments of spines or pedicellariae, have to rely on concealment or on the rather forlorn hope of flight to avoid their attackers. Slow-moving though they are, they may be successful in escaping from similarly ponderous enemies. For instance, the cake-urchins and heart-urchins with their small, close-lying spines of little use for protection, burrow into the sand or mud, usually quite out of sight. In some places they are hunted by carnivorous marine snails that dig in search of them. Once the snail gets a foothold on the echinoid it can rasp a small hole in the test with its minute, file-like series of teeth and extract the soft internal organs through the hole by inserting its proboscis. Some observations on the West Indian heart-urchin *Plagiobrissus grandis* (Plate IX, fig. d), made by skin diving, include the observation that 'Several shells that were almost buried were removed with urchins clasped in the fore part of the foot. One urchin that had escaped was seen trundling along on its short spines with a large *Cassis* (the snail) in hot pursuit. Evidently this was an exception, as no other fugitives were seen. The result of the chase was not observed but the heart-urchin seemed to be making good his escape.'[1] Some starfishes, such as *Luidia* and various Astropectinids, also feed on these irregular echinoids, particularly the cake-urchins. One big West Indian *Luidia* with a diameter of nearly 30 cm. was found dead with a cake-urchin of the genus *Mellita*, almost six cm. across, stuck inside its mouth. The soft parts of the *Mellita* had been digested but the test was still intact.

The holothurians, despite their lack of solid armament, derive a measure of protection from their thick, leathery, sometimes slippery skins. A moderate-sized starfish of the voracious species *Pycnopodia helianthoides*, has been seen manoeuvering for several hours trying to swallow a smooth holothurian of the genus *Stichopus* (a relative of *Holothuria*) heavier than itself, but failing since its tube feet could get no purchase.[2]

[1] Moore, *Nautilus*, vol. 69, pp. 73–76, 1956.
[2] Fisher, *Bull. U.S. National Museum*, vol. 76, 1928.

Some Echinoderms with good powers of regeneration can mutilate themselves deliberately to escape the clutches of a predator, casting off part or the whole of an arm or even jettisoning a larger portion of the body. The easily broken syzygial joints of crinoids particularly allow for such seizures or other damage, likewise the brittle arm-joints of many brittle-stars. Echinoids and holothurians with their more compact body forms have not developed this facility, but certain holothurians, such as the British *Holothuria forskali*, use their powers of regeneration in another way. When attacked, they bend the hind part of the body around in the direction of the threat and squirt some thin white threads through the anus. These threads swell up and elongate to form a sticky mass, serving to distract or even to entangle the predator. The threads are really blind-ending tubules (called the Cuvierian tubules after the French biologist Cuvier). They are developed within the body cavity at the posterior end. Their ejection involves an actual rupture of the tissue near their point of attachment, caused by a powerful contraction of the body wall, while pressure from the body cavity is believed to account for their enormous elongation once in the water. The action is irreversible, the tubules once ejected becoming detached from the body and later regenerated. This defensive habit has led to the popular name of the cotton-spinner for *H. forskali*. A more drastic total evisceration occurs in a number of holothurians when in dire straits, the gut and its associated organs being forced out. Here again regeneration follows if the holothurian survives.

In recent years a new kind of poison has been discovered in a number of holothurians, particularly in their body walls. This has been called holothurin. Its presence accounts for the death of fishes and other animals put in aquaria previously occupied by these holothurians. This lethal property has been known for some time by natives of certain Pacific islands. They make a practice of putting mashed or cut-up holothurians into coral reef pools to bring fishes to the surface in a semi-paralysed condition. The poison does not seem to affect man, since some of the Japanese Pacific islanders are not deterred from eating the same species of holothurian which they use on the fishes, though it is not one of the more prized kinds of edible sea-cucumber. Possibly the preparation of the holothurians or beche-der-mer as human food by repeated boiling helps to nullify any toxic effect, but two species of beche-de-mer are apparently eaten raw in Japan and these proved to be among the 80 per cent of the Japanese holothurian species tested which were found by experiment to be poisonous to fishes in some degree.

PARASITES AND COMMENSALS

In discussing live animals it is always desirable to consider them against the background of the other organisms, both plant and animal, which share their habitat, that is as part of the whole community. Apart from their relationships as predators or as prey, which have already been dealt with, Echinoderms live in a balanced state approaching mutual tolerance with a number of other animals and plants, as long as the prevailing conditions are almost unchanged. Should conditions alter and the balance be upset, then this tolerance may break down in certain directions. For instance, if the food of one animal in the community becomes scarce then it may start to compete for an alternative source of food, just as foxes turned more to poultry when rabbits became rare in England owing to myxomatosis.

There are also physically closer relationships between individuals of different species. In any association there is a balance of advantage and disadvantage between the participants. If this is heavily weighted on one side, then it is a case of parasitism; the partner getting all the benefit is the parasite, while the one of which advantage is being taken is the host. On the other hand, when the balance is nearly even and the advantages are mutual, the condition is called symbiosis. Between these two extremes come many associations where one partner gets more benefit but at the same time the other does not suffer unduly; these are instances of commensalism. Of course there are many borderline cases between parasitism and commensalism for which an exact definition is controversial. This is complicated by the fact that some external parasites (as opposed to internal ones living within the tissues of the host), particularly those that simply steal some of the host's food, may do little harm if there are only a few of them present, though in large numbers they may be a serious drain on the food supply.

The only Echinoderms which might be called parasites are tropical brittle-stars of the genus *Ophiomaza*, related to *Ophiothrix*. They are commonly found clinging on to the upper surfaces of feather-stars and helping themselves to the food collected by their hosts as it passes along the ambulacral grooves to the mouth. Since the crinoid probably does not suffer, as long as the food supply is abundant, and the brittle-stars only occur singly, as far as we know, this association might instead be termed commensal rather than parasitic.

Ophiomaza is one of the few brittle-stars with arm joints capable of flexing downwards, not just sideways. This allows it to embrace the disc of the crinoid from above without hampering the free movement of the crinoid's arms. Such an arm joint is also found in the related genera *Ophiothrix* and *Ophiothela*, and is not a special modification evolved with the parasitic habit. *Ophiomaza* itself seems to have no obvious physical adaptations in connection with its habit and could probably live apart from its host, whereas a more specialized parasite could not.

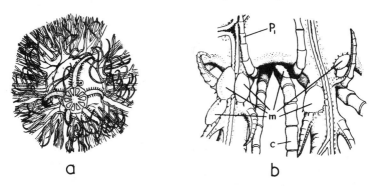

a b

Fig. 27. a) Upper side of the disc and arm bases of the tropical feather-star *Comanthus* with the brittle-star *Ophiomaza*, matching in colour, parasitic upon it; *Comanthus* belongs to the family Comasteridae and so has the mouth offset towards the edge of the disc, also the arms on the opposite side from the mouth have their ambulacral grooves reduced, b) upper side of the edge of the disc and two arm bases of *Antedon bifida* showing six myzostomes parasitic upon it

An interesting parallel to the habit of *Ophiomaza* is shown by a few other brittle-stars, notably one called *Ophiodaphne materna*. The two sexes of this species differ considerably in size. The male is a dwarf, its disc diameter being no more than a fifth that of the female. In addition, the two sexes pair up at an early stage; each female carries a diminutive male on its lower side, their arms alternating and their mouths and genital openings facing each other. The specific name *materna* is a mis-nomer brought about by the dried condition of the specimens on which the species was based, so that the sex difference went undiscovered and the faulty conclusion was reached that the small specimens were young ones being reared by their mothers. The dwarfing of the male sex and its modification to the habit of parasitizing the female to some extent, occurs sporadically throughout the animal kingdom, perhaps the best known example being that of the angler fishes, where the tiny male becomes fused on to the body of the female. In the case of these brittle-stars the degree of parasitism is not so marked although it is improbable that the males can survive apart from their consorts.

The vulnerability of the feeding method in feather-stars has resulted in their exploitation by a number of other parasites, notably some peculiar Annelid worms called Myzostomes. These are quite unlike normal worms in form, having the body almost discoidal and rather flat. *Myzostomum cirriferum*, which occurs on *Antedon bifida* in European waters, resembles a little rounded scale, with the upper side slightly convex; around the edge are ten pairs of 'cirri' and there are five pairs of processes or parapodia on the ventral side armed at their tips with hooks.

Myzostomes like this creep about on the disc and arms of feather-stars, rather like a flea on a dog. To feed, each one extends its proboscis into the ambulacral grooves of the feather-star to intercept the particles of food and mucus as they are carried along towards the mouth by the ciliary current.

The frequency of these parasites varies in different localities; they may be rare in some places so that most of the feather-stars in a population escape being infested with them, while elsewhere they are more numerous. Some Scandinavian specimens of *Antedon* have been found each harbouring several hundred myzostomes.

There are also species of myzostomes that are less active; these either stay in one place on the host or else burrow into its tissues so that the feather-star is induced to develop a gall around them (figs. 28c and d). If the gall is in a pinnule, it may cause the segments distal to it to become deformed.

Still other myzostomes penetrate into the body cavity or digestive tract of their host. Such internally parasitic myzostomes also infest certain starfishes and brittle-stars, though the Echinoderms other than feather-stars are more subject to crustacean and molluscan parasites. However, a few of the more usual kinds of marine worms also associate with various Echinoderms as mild parasites or commensals. This is particularly true in the starfishes, several of which are commonly found with one or more worms living amongst the spines on their ventral sides or lying along the ambulacral grooves. These worms intercept the smaller particles of food being carried over the surface to the mouth. *Astropecten irregularis* of British waters often harbours the worm *Acholoë squamosa* (formerly known as *Acholoë astericola*). If there are several worms on one starfish, then the largest usually lies along one of the grooves. It may even put its head into the mouth of the *Astropecten* and take food from the stomach, which is almost incredible since *Astropecten* is primarily carnivorous. The same species of worm will also associate with *Luidia* and a few other starfishes but not with *Asterias* or other Forcipulates, possibly because of their more mobile, numerous and better developed pedicellariae. A related genus of worm, *Harmothoë*, shares the burrow of various larger animals that feed on small particles by means of ciliary currents, including heart-urchins such as *Echinocardium* and brittle-stars such as *Acrocnida*, a large British Amphiurid.

There are even a few brittle-stars that are themselves commensal with cake-urchins. One of these, called *Nannophiura*, a real pygmy with a disc no more than half a millimetre across, climbs about on the urchin's spines using its prehensile arms almost like a monkey in the trees.

Among the burrowing holothurians, certain Synaptids including *Leptosynapta* are associated with some peculiar kinds of bivalve molluscs. One of these, *Entovalva mirabilis*, lives in the intestine of its host, but a related Japanese form, *Devonia semperi*, has an extraordinary development of the foot into a large disc-like suction-cup, more like a snail's foot, with which it clings on to the outside of the Synaptid *Protankyra*. Some less specialized bivalves live in the burrows of certain heart-urchins such as *Echinocardium* and *Spatangus*.

The real parasites among molluscs, however, are certain kinds of true snails. These are mostly small, less than a quarter of an inch in length. Some may attach themselves to the outside of the host, feeding on the external tissues, or bore through the body wall with the proboscis, while others burrow into the surface, sometimes inducing the development of a gall, or even penetrating into the body cavity. The internal parasites, as usual, are more degenerate in form and more specialized for reproduction than the external parasites. A very degraded parasitic snail, *Parenteroxenos dogieli*, lives inside the holothurian *Cucumaria japonica*; it has no shell and no internal organs except for the reproductive ones, while its shape is worm-like and much coiled, since it may reach the surprising length of over a meter, the host being only a few centimeters long.

Many of the parasitic crustaceans too are extraordinarily degenerate, notably those, such as *Dendrogaster*, which are related to the barnacles. As the name suggests, these form lobed or branching masses in the body cavity of the host and their affinities are only revealed by the barnacle-type larva that they produce. These degenerate barnacles are mainly found in starfishes and brittle-stars among the Echinoderms but also occur in some sea-urchins. A Danish worker estimated that over half the specimens of the heart-urchin *Echinocardium* living in the vicinity of Copenhagen are probably infected with parasites of this kind, their sac-like bodies lying inside the test and connecting with the water

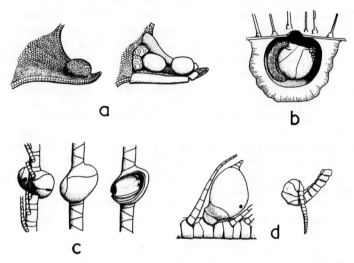

Fig. 28. a) Distorted arm of the antarctic starfish *Acodontaster* intact and cut open to show two cyst-like parasitic crustaceans, each of which has an opening on the ventral side of the host; the inner one of the two was concealed in external view by the arching of the disc of the starfish, b) a gall on the inside of the ventral wall of the test of the sea-urchin *Hygrosoma petersi* cut open to show the parasitic copepod inside [after Bonnier], c) a gall produced on the arm of a feather-star in two views and cut open to show the large female and very small male (top right) parasitic myzostomes inside and d) galls on the pinnules of two feather-stars showing different kinds of distortion. [c) and d) after von Graaff]

outside by a pore to allow the escape of the larvae. Such parasites may damage the gonads of the host, sea-urchin or starfish, and in extreme cases may even castrate it, in the same way that the related parasite *Sacculina* unsexes the common shore crab. In some starfishes the larvae of the parasites first get into the body cavity of the host through the thin-walled respiratory papulae. The related parasites in brittle-stars are not so degenerate and even when fully developed their crustacean affinities are evident.

Also important among the crustaceans as parasites are the copepods, a group of small, mainly planktonic forms that make up a large part of the food of fishes like the herring. Some of these, such as *Ophioika* found in the brittle-star *Ophiacantha*, are very degenerate as adults, with a lobed body, but most of them still have some visible appendages and joints, though their body-form is often very swollen. It is only while they are larvae that these highly modified copepods can infect their hosts. With starfishes they occur mainly as relatively unmodified external parasites but in associating with brittle-stars some of them penetrate into the genital bursae or even into the body cavity, sometimes inducing the host to form a gall around them. Similar parasitic copepods also cause galls in some sea-urchins, particularly inside the thin-walled tests of Echinothuriids (fig. 28b) and at the bases of the spines of these and other echinoids.

A number of other crustaceans live commensally with various Echinoderms, gaining food and some degree of protection from the association. Certain prawns and shrimps which live on tropical featherstars and on the sea-urchin *Echinometra* are interesting since they have developed a protective coloration to match the colours and patterns of their particular hosts. However, the only internal parasites, apart from the copepods and relatives of barnacles already mentioned, are some small types of crabs. One of these, *Pinnaxodes*, invades the rectum of several species of sea-urchins that live in Chile, Peru and Ecuador, entering through the anus when young. Since the crab grows to a size of nearly an inch across the shell, the rectum of the host becomes distorted and the crab is imprisoned within the test, just as if it were in a gall. The tips of its claws may be visible through the anus and in one kind of sea-urchin the upper part of the test is deformed by the parasite inside. One species of *Pinnaxodes* and a few related crabs have also been found in the cloaca of certain Chilean and other Pacific holothurians. Apart from the discomforting presence of the crabs within their bodies, the Echinoderms are probably little affected, and this sort of association might be called a commensal one. Surprisingly enough, there are some small fishes that similarly invade the cloaca of holothurians, usually entering tail first. One of these, *Carapus*, grows to a length of about six inches so that its tail projects into the respiratory trees that lead off the cloaca and its head may show at the anus. This fish can probably live successfully apart from the holothurian and it seems to have no special sense enabling it to find its host at a distance, unlike many other parasites or commensals such as the worms that live on *Astropecten* and *Luidia*.

Another fish of a similar kind lives actually in the body cavity of the big thick tropical starfish *Culcita* (Plate V, fig. h). How it gets there is uncertain but it most probably enters through the mouth and stomach wall of the host.

In addition, the Echinoderms are subject to infestation by many of the ordinary kinds of internal parasites such as ciliate protozoans, flat-worms and round-worms. Some of these are more or less harmful but, like other parasites, their effects are rarely fatal, since their own survival depends on the survival of the host.

Finally, there are more haphazard associations where one animal simply grows on or lives on the surface of a larger one, just as if it was an inanimate part of the sea-floor. For instance, a variety of marine growths such as barnacles, sponges and tube-worms, often encrust the large primary spines of the cidarid sea-urchins (Plate VIII, fig. a). These are able to settle because the fully grown spines lose their protective skin covering, unlike the spines of most sea-urchins. In this sort of association, the smaller organism is said to be epizoic on the larger one. Some ophiuroids are epizoic on such creatures as sea-fans and sponges (Plate VII, fig. g), though the association of a few kinds of brittle-stars with cake-urchins verges on a commensal one since the brittle-star takes a share of the edible detritus in the sand flowing over the cake-urchin as it ploughs along.

HABITS AND BEHAVIOUR

All echinoderms, except for a very few swimming holothurians, live at the bottom of the sea. Even those like the brittle-stars which can travel quite fast, spend much of their time in one place, only moving when stimulated into action by hunger or adversity. Such a sedentary way of life has discouraged the evolution of complex patterns of behaviour, while the decentralized nature of the nervous system coupled with the radial form also tend to prohibit this. Apart from the holothurians and the irregular echinoids, which do have a distinct front end, nearly all Echinoderms can move in any direction horizontally with any of the arms or rays leading. Sometimes too the foremost part may be interradial since the five-armed brittle-stars can move either with the odd arm trailing behind or with it in front. However, once a part of the body has taken the lead, it usually retains it until progress is checked, when its dominance is soon lost. Should the Echinoderm be stimulated later to move in a new direction, then the arm or ray that happens to be nearest will usually take over the lead. As already described in the chapter on orientation, a few species, such as the Pacific many-armed starfish *Pycnopodia*, are exceptional in this respect, since they will revolve after being checked in one direction and move off in another with the same arm still in the lead.

So far, there is little evidence that Echinoderms have any but the feeblest sense of purpose in their activities. They seem to move at random and few sustain their efforts in any one direction for long, or resume them determinedly after interruption. At the same time their capacity for learning is poor, though one experimenter found that starfishes forced to use certain arms each time they righted themselves when overturned, would continue to use these same arms for each consecutive effort for up to five days after they were left free following each upturning.

'Righting'

The 'righting' reaction in Echinoderms has been a favourite study for a long time, since the necessity of keeping the feet on the ground seems to be a basic one, and a healthy specimen will always try to regain its normal position. Also the reaction in starfishes is particularly interesting because of the variety of methods of righting used, some of them more efficient than others. After being overturned there is usually a short interval, then the starfish begins to bend the tips of its arms underneath, or to twist them sideways so that the terminal podia or feet can make contact with the bottom. In the most generally used somersault method of righting, when two or three arm tips have got a grip, they start to walk inwards under the body, while the unattached arms either swing over vertically or fold over to lie above the attached ones in the horizontal plane, and then crawl off on to the substrate (figs. 29a and b). Sometimes a starfish will foul itself up by getting a grip with more than three of the arms so that it cannot somersault or fold over until at least two have let go. Consequently the time taken in righting varies considerably even with one individual, while the rate for different specimens and species depends on their size and agility and

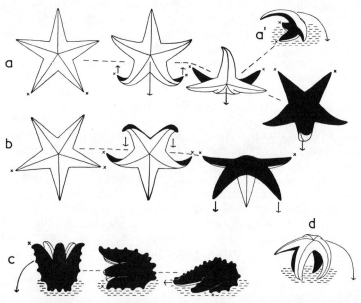

Fig. 29. Diagrams of starfishes to show some of the different ways in which they right themselves after being turned upside down; a) and b) viewed from above, c) and d) from the side. a) Four stages of a somersault on two arms, with a′) the third stage seen in side view, with all but the uppermost arm foreshortened, b) three stages of a folding turn, c) three stages of a 'tulip' turn and d) an inverted 'tulip' turn, one arm having detached itself from the bottom to swing the centre of gravity over to the right. a), b) and d) are of an *Astropecten* and c) of a *Protoreaster*. Both folding and somersaulting may also be done using different combinations and numbers of arms [Partly after Tortonese and Ohshima].

the relative rigidity of their skeletons. The most agile ones can right themselves in less than ten seconds, while large and stiff species may take anything from several minutes to several hours; the average is probably two or three minutes.

The 'tulip' method of righting is a variation of folding, used particularly by relatively stiff species like the big Oreasterid *Protoreaster nodosus*. While lying on its back the starfish raises all its arms into a more or less vertical position and then rolls over on to one side so that the uppermost arms are the right way up (as in folding) and can crawl off the inverted lower ones. The 'inverted tulip' method is the reverse of this since it starts like the somersault with the arm tips arching underneath, but the centre of the body is then raised so high that the arms become almost vertical with their tips still on the bottom. After toppling over to one side the starfish can easily straighten out. This method is sometimes used by *Astropecten* and others with no sucking discs on the tube feet, though they may also somersault or fold instead.

The very short-armed and bulky starfish *Culcita* (Plate V, fig. h) manages to right by partially inflating itself at one side so that the ventral surface is tilted and the terminal feet of the lower rays can get a grip to start a somersault. Sea-urchins with their even more nearly spherical and rigid bodies do not have the same difficulty since their tube feet extend on to the upper surface and can immediately get a grip to start them rolling over and bring the mouth down towards the substrate again. However, flattened cake-urchins which have the dorsal podia reduced can only turn over by burrowing themselves laboriously down into the sand; on a hard surface they would be helpless. The very mobile and prehensile arms of brittle-stars and feather-stars, and the flexible rounded bodies of holothurians, simplify the problem of righting for them.

Experiments with starfishes have shown that only those like *Pycnopodia*, with a dominant arm that leads in whichever direction they move, also tend to right themselves using the same arm or arms each time.

As in ordinary locomotion, the righting reaction needs the co-ordination of all the arms and becomes almost impossible if the nerve ring connecting the radial nerves of the individual arms is cut in each interradius; though an isolated arm of some starfishes (or a sector of the test of a sea-urchin) is capable of righting itself independently if it is severed from the body (as long as it remains healthy of course).

Reactions to light

Some other reactions of Echinoderms can be completed even when the nerve ring is damaged. For instance, the defensive pointing of spines at any threatening shadow in sea-urchins such as *Diadema*, involves connection of the muscles at the bases of the spines through the radial nerve to light sensitive cells scattered all over the surface. At one time it was thought that the blue 'eye spots' of *Diadema* were centres of light sensitivity but this supposition has been disproved.[1] Not only does *Diadema* have a quick response to shading but also it is one of the very few Echinoderms able to change its colour by night and day, though this ability is reduced in older specimens. Black pigment in large cells in the skin becomes diffused in bright light so that the colour of the whole sea-urchin is dark. When night falls the pigment is concentrated in small patches and the general colour lightens. If a *Diadema* accustomed to the light is suddenly put in the dark, within an hour or two it will become quite pale. However, a specimen accustomed to the light but then shaded will move to a nearby light area if possible. Similarly, if it is accustomed to the dark it will usually return to it. The habit of colour change with the passage of day and night is so strong that specimens brought into the dark and kept there will continue to change their colour to some extent at the appropriate times for several days before losing their rhythm.

In starfishes, besides a general sensitivity of the body surface to light intensity, there are special organs like rudimentary compound eyes called optic cushions. One of these lies at the tip of each arm near the base of the unpaired sensory terminal tube foot, appearing as a small red spot. This colour is due to the presence of pigment cells in the walls of the minute cup-shaped ocelli that are scattered all over the cushion. Also the ocelli have sensory retinal cells in their walls, and sometimes the epidermis roofing them over is thickened like a lens to concentrate the light rays. Just how much the starfish can appreciate the shape of nearby objects with these organs has not yet been estimated. Some starfishes like *Astropecten* have simpler optic cushions with no pigment cups and the retinal cells are scattered.

Except for a few Synaptid holothurians which have light-sensitive organs at the bases of the tentacles, other Echinoderms have only the general system of photosensory cells all over the surface. Some of the species that live in the deep sea where no light penetrates have lost this faculty altogether.

The activity of many shallow-water Echinoderms varies with the light intensity, so that the ability to appreciate this is important. One Indo-Pacific species of *Astropecten* is active only in the half light at dawn and dusk, remaining buried in the sand for the rest of the time. Some others are nocturnal. *Diadema* for instance rarely exposes itself

[1] Millott, *Phil. Trans. Roy. Soc.*, vol. 238 B, pp. 187–220, 1954.

to the full tropical midday sun but lurks in crevices and other shady places until dark, when it comes out into the open and moves about in search of food. *Paracentrotus lividus*, so common on the rocky shores of the Mediterranean, may be found in large numbers in the daytime fully exposed in only a few inches of water. However, this species, like the British *Psammechinus* at low water level, is often found shading itself with bits of weed or debris held above it by the upper tube feet.

Burrowing

Paracentrotus is also interesting because in some places, where it is liable to be dislodged by the action of waves, it actually burrows into the rock to form a cavity for itself by the abrading action of the spines, possibly aided by the teeth. The power of this burrowing ability has been demonstrated by a remarkable discovery[1] on the Californian coast of some steel pier piles three-eights of an inch thick, which, after twenty years in the water, had been completely perforated in places. This was accounted for by the presence of sea-urchins of the genus *Strongylocentrotus*, many of them found in hollows in the piles made shiny by their scraping action, the anti-corrosive surface layer being worn away, exposing the steel to the leaching effect of the sea-water, as well as to further wear by the urchins' spines. The most efficient echinoid rock borer is probably an Indo-Pacific species called *Echinostrephus molaris*. This sea-urchin makes a cylindrical hole several inches deep, into which it fits very snugly and can wedge itself tightly with its spines so that extraction is almost impossible. For much of the time *Echinostrephus* stays at the entrance to its burrow ready to drop down into it at the least sign of danger.

Burrowing into soft surfaces is a very common habit among Echinoderms and is found in all the major groups, except for the crinoids which need to keep their food grooves clear. Many brittle-stars, particularly of the family Amphiuridae, sink the body vertically into the sand or mud, using the podia as scoops, until all but the arm tips are covered (fig. 30d). The exposed parts of the arms sweep about above the surface and catch up particles of detritus for food. At the same time a respiratory current is produced through the burrow around the body, possibly assisted by pumping movements of the disc of the brittle-star. The burrow itself is formed with the aid of a mucous secretion to cement the particles of sand together.

Mucus is also important in forming the burrows of heart-urchins. Some of them, like *Echinocardium cordatum* found on the British coast

[1] Irwin, *Science*, vol. 118, p. 307, 1953.

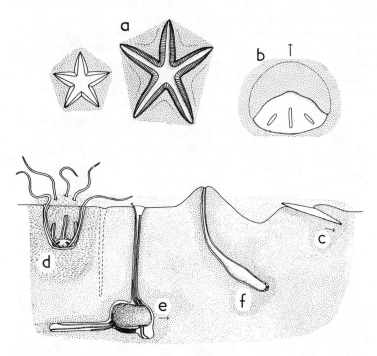

Fig. 30. Burrowing positions of certain Echinoderms; a) and b) seen from above, c) to f) imaginary views from the side in their burrows. a) Normal outline (left) of *Astropecten marginatus* for comparison with (right) a specimen in the act of burying itself, with the sides of the arms and disc bent upwards so that the edges of the infero-marginal plates are visible; the sand is being piled interradially by the excavating action of the tube feet below, b) the cake-urchin *Mellita* burying itself and c) the same from the side, d) amphiurid brittle-star in its muddy burrow (the others are in sand), e) the heart-urchin *Echinocardium cordatum* with a few tube feet shown, two feeding ones from near the mouth and the others maintaining the respiratory and excretory tubes in the sand; behind is shown the previous respiratory tube, now filled in, f) the holothurian *Paracaudina*, showing the hollow in the sand left by a quantity of it having been swallowed and the cone formed around the tip of the extended 'tail' by the sand discharged. [a) and b) after photographs of Kenk, d) after Thorson, e) after Nichols and f) after Yamanouchi]

at low water spring tide level and beyond, dig themselves in almost vertically, mainly by the use of their lateral spines. The depth that they reach depends on their size and on the consistency of the sand, but is often as much as 20 cm. below the surface, or several times their own height. By means of the enormously extensible tube feet of the frontal ambulacrum on the dorsal side, a temporary respiratory tube is formed. It leads vertically up to the surface of the sand and its wall is cemented by mucus (fig. 30e). At the same time the subanal tube feet maintain a horizontal tube extending sometimes more than ten cm. from the posterior end of the urchin and allowing for the disposal of the waste products from the anus. Both these tubes tend to fall in, particularly in loose sand, so that the feet have to repair them continually. Once it is buried, *Echinocardium* ploughs slowly forward through the sand when feeding, using the paddle-shaped ventral spines to push itself along. The far end of the subanal tube falls in as it gets beyond the reach of the feet, but the vertical respiratory tube is soon abandoned altogether and replaced by a new one further forward. Another British species, *Spatangus purpureus*, makes a much more shallow burrow; it lives in loose shell gravel rather than fine sand and only goes an inch or two below the surface, so it does not need to maintain a special respiratory tube.[1]

The flattened cake-urchins do not burrow down vertically but plough their way forwards and downwards into the sand by a combined wave action of their many fine spines. As they slide under it the sand becomes banked up in front and over them. Most species bury themselves completely, but the Californian *Dendraster* leaves its hind end sticking out.

Many holothurians, particularly those with the tube feet reduced or absent, also burrow 'head' first, but like the worms they do it by muscular contractions of the body wall. *Paracaudina* rests in a sloping burrow with its 'head' down and the slender 'tail' reaching up to the surface. *Leptosynapta* is another that buries itself 'head' first but it keeps on the move like an earthworm and does not maintain any special position for long. *Thyone*, unlike these others, only buries the middle part of its body, which it does by shuffling straight down with muscular contractions. This is a very laborious method and takes several hours, whereas *Leptosynapta* can bury itself completely in only five minutes.

Among the echinoids, *Echinocardium* usually take fifteen minutes or more to burrow out of sight, but cake-urchins such as *Mellita* may do it in one to three minutes, according to size; some other cake-urchins are slower, needing ten minutes or more to conceal themselves.

[1] Nichols, *Phil. Trans. Roy. Soc.*, vol. 242B, pp. 347–437, 1959.

A starfish like the flattened West Indian *Astropecten marginatus* can get below the surface in about a minute by flexing the sides of the arms and disc upwards so that each arm becomes V-shaped in cross-section and the large tube feet can shovel the sand grains away sideways to allow the starfish to sink straight down.

Many of these burrowing Echinoderms, as well as others which live exposed on the bottom, are often found in amazing numbers in localities where conditions are particularly suitable for them. Various species of *Amphiura* and genera related to it are dominant members of the animal communities of many muddy areas at depths of about 20 fathoms in all parts of the world. In exceptionally dense populations there may be more than 1000 Amphiurids in one square meter. The number of other kinds of animals that make up the fauna of such areas is rather limited, but there are usually some bivalved molluscs, various worms and heart-urchins. Where the substrate tends to be more sandy *Echinocardium* will occur, but if it is silty there will be other genera instead.

When studying communities of those brittle-stars such as *Ophiothrix*, which live exposed on the surface of harder substrates (usually gravel in this case), the numbers can be estimated by photography.[1] In some places a few miles off the coast near Plymouth, photographs show a seething mass of these brittle-stars so close together that their arms overlap. There may be two or three hundred in one square meter or over a million per acre, and the patches where they occur may be several square miles in extent. In some colder areas of the north Pacific and Arctic oceans, certain feather-stars may also be dredged up in vast numbers, particularly in parts of the sea where the currents renew the water constantly and the organic detritus from dead and dying plankton sinking to the bottom provides a plentiful supply of food.

[1] Vevers, *Journ. Mar. biol. Assn.*, vol. 31, pp. 215–222, 1952.

LIFE SPAN

The life spans of several different Echinoderms have been studied; they seem to average about four years. *Asterias rubens* is one of the longer-lived, often surviving for five or six years, though *Luidia ciliaris* lives for only three or four. Large specimens of *Echinus esculentus* are said to be four to eight years old but *Echinocardium cordatum* probably lives to only three. *Ophiura texturata* also seems to have a short span, of between two and three years. The time that each species takes to become sexually mature also varies. While some reach this condition within the first year others take two or three.

SPAWNING HABITS

Spawning, or shedding of the eggs and sperm is usually limited to a few months of the year in any one species, particularly the spring and early summer months for those living in shallow temperate seas. A few have an even more restricted period. Almost the entire population of the crinoid *Comanthus japonicus* spawns during the afternoon of a day in early October when the moon is half full. A few sea-urchins have also been observed spawning at certain phases of the moon, but such habits are exceptional. In some species each individual only spawns once a year but in others the discharge may be repeated at intervals over a period.

The behaviour at spawning time is often very modified, particularly with burrowing Echinoderms. *Amphiura*, for instance, arches its body up out of the mud with its arms buried, in a reversal of its usual posture, while *Leptosynapta* swings the front part of its body about above the surface.

In only one starfish genus, the tropical Indo-Pacific *Archaster*, are the males and females known to associate at spawning time. During the breeding season they are often found in pairs, a male on top of a female, with their arms alternating. The sperm is probably shed into the water as with other starfishes, but there is a much better chance that most of the eggs will be fertilized than with the haphazard shedding of other Echinoderms.

ECONOMIC INTEREST

Echinoderms are only of limited interest from the economic point of view, particularly in England at the present day. A few of them, notably brittle-stars, are of some value as food for fishes like the lemon sole and cod, though they are not usually the main source. On the harmful side, some starfishes are pests of oyster and mussel beds, though their nuisance value is probably less than that of other predators such as the whelk tingle, a mollusc, and investigations[1] in south-east England at least, suggest that the starfishes show some preference for eating instead the slipper-limpet *Crepidula*, which itself is a nuisance on oyster beds since it competes with the oysters for the same kind of food.

In the eastern United States, the menace to oysters and scallops is more serious and several experiments have been carried out to try to find an economic use for dead starfishes collected either by dragging large mops over the oyster beds, or more recently by skin divers. Unfortunately their use in agricultural fertilizers or as chicken food does not seem to be a commercial proposition, taking into account the costs of collection, preparation and marketing and the irregularity of supply.

In the past, the roes of the big sea-urchin *Echinus esculentus* were often used as food in coastal districts of England. Sea-urchins of various species are still marketed commercially in a few parts of the world, notably in Brittany and on the Mediterranean coast of France, as well as in Italy, Greece and further afield in the West Indies at the island of Barbados, on the west coast of South America and in Japan and Malaya. In Europe the favourite kind of roe is that of *Paracentrotus*, though a few other species are also collected. Not all urchins are edible and the Mediterranean *Arbacia*, which is superficially rather like *Paracentrotus*, is rejected. In Barbados the sea-urchins (*Tripneustes*) are collected by skin divers with hand nets (and presumably calloused hands), brought to the beach where the shells are broken open and the roes of about a dozen specimens are packed into one shell, covered over with a leaf and sold at fourpence each (at least that was the controlled price in 1948). In some places the roes are boiled or baked, but in others they are eaten raw with various additions, such as lemon juice.

A more important industry based on Echinoderms as a source of food is the beche-de-mer or trepang fishery, carried on mainly in the Indo-Pacific. These names are of French and Malay origin and are collective terms for certain sea-cucumbers of the order Aspidochirota

[1] Hancock, *Journ. Mar. biol. Assn.*, vol. 34, pp. 313–331, 1955.

—that is *Holothuria* and its relatives. Though now abandoned in areas like northern Australia, where it was once an important side-line of the pearl-shell fishery, the collection and marketing of beche-de-mer is still widespread, to satisfy the demand of many oriental people. Various species of sea-cucumber are used. One of the most prized belongs to the genus *Actinopyga* and is called 'red-fish' in Australia, 'Hung-Hur' by the Chinese and 'Oe Liow' in the Philippine Islands; about the year 1930 it fetched a price of about £200 a ton in Queensland.

A few of the smaller kinds of beche-de-mer are eaten raw in salads but usually the cucumbers are split open, gutted, boiled (often repeatedly) and then dried or smoked until reduced to a shrivelled, almost rigid condition, convenient for transport and sale. To make them edible they are soaked, then chopped or minced and made into soup, but sometimes may be roasted and eaten whole instead.

About 1935 an attempt was made in Italy to utilize several different Mediterranean species of holothurians commercially, either for eating from cans, like sardines, or in powdered form. This industry had to contend with the high costs of using European workers as well as the necessity of building up a market for its own products.

The only other use of Echinoderms which may be mentioned here, though hardly an economic one, is that of their eggs as subjects for fundamental laboratory research on cell structure, fertilization and experimental embryology. In recent years sea-urchin eggs have even been shot into space in rockets to find out whether cosmic rays or other such phenomena have any effect on living organisms.

Clearly the uses of Echinoderms are few and not very important and their potentialities are restricted in range. Nevertheless, they are a fascinating group to study, not only for their obvious artistic appeal, but also as a specialized offshoot in the evolution of the animal kingdom.

SUGGESTED FURTHER READING

BOOLOOTIAN, R. A. (Editor). *Physiology of Echinodermata.* xviii+822 pp., figs. Interscience Publishers, New York, etc., 1966.

HYMAN, L. H. *The Invertebrates*, vol. 4, *Echinodermata*, 763 pp., 280 figs. McGraw-Hill, New York, 1955.

MILLOTT, N. (Editor). Echinoderm Biology. *Symp. zool. Soc. Lond.* No. 20: xiv+240, figs., 1967.

MOORE, R. C. (Editor). Treatise on Invertebrate Paleontology. Parts S & U. Echinodermata 1 & 3. Pp. 650 & 695. Geological Society of America Inc.: University of Kansas Press. 1966, 1967.

MORTENSEN, T. *Handbook of the Echinoderms of the British Isles,* 471 pp., 269 figs. Oxford University Press, London, 1927.

NICHOLS, D. *Echinoderms.* (Revd. edit.). 200 pp., 26 figs. Hutchinson University Library, London, 1966.

Index

Page numbers set in *italic* type refer to illustrations.

157

Psammechinus, 31, 147
Pseudocolochirus axiologus, 105
Psolus, 83, 86, 89
   chitonoides, 104
   diomediae, 87, 89
   squamatus, 89
Psychropotes longicauda, 87
Pteraster, 55, 59, 62, *62*
   tesselatus, 40
Ptilocrinus, 91, 94
Pycnopodia, 22, 130, 133, 143, 145
   helianthoides, 110, 134

Rhizocrinus, 92, 94, 98, 102
   lofotensis, 90, 102
Rhopalocidaris, 80
Rhopalodina, 83, 86
Rhopiella, 55
Rotula, 76, *77*

Scotoplanes globosa, 87
Solaster, 59, 111

papposus, 15, *16*
Spatangus, 77, 78, 79, 139
   purpureus, 149
Sperosoma giganteum, 76
Stichopus, 134
   variegatus, 100
Strongylocentrotus, 121, 130, 147
   franciscanus, 97
Styracaster, 63
Synapta, 88
   maculata, 86
Synaptula, 84, *84*

Thaumatocrinus, 92
Thyone, 149
Tosia, 11, 12, 50, *51*, 62, *62*
Toxopneustes, 80, *80*, *117*, 132, *133*
Trichaster, 66
Tripneustes, 73, 74, 153

Zygometra microdiscus, 95

160